YEARBOOK 2009/10

Supported by
ARTS COUNCIL ENGLAND

First published in 2009 by the Royal Opera House in association with Oberon Books Ltd

Oberon Books
521 Caledonian Road, London N7 9RH
Tel 020 7607 3637 Fax 020 7607 3629
info@oberonbooks.com
www.oberonbooks.com

Cover and book design: Jeff Willis

Project Manager: Will Richmond

Editor: Stephen Watson

Royal Opera House Commissioning Editor: John Snelson

Every effort has been made to trace the copyright holders of all images reprinted in this book. Acknowledgement is made in all cases where the image source is available, but we would be grateful for information about any images where sources could not be traced.

A catalogue record for this book is available from the British Library.

ISBN 987-1-84002-939-0

Printed and bound in Great Britain by CPI Antony Rowe, Chippenham.

Royal Opera House
Covent Garden
London WC2E 9DD
Box Office 020 7304 4000
www.roh.org.uk

Front cover: Melissa Hamilton and Eric Underwood in Infra.
Photograph: Bill Cooper
Back cover: Dancers of The Royal Ballet in Diamonds.
Photograph: Bill Cooper
Inside front cover and title page: Dancers of The Royal Ballet in Diamonds. *Photograph: Bill Cooper*
Inside back cover: Dancers of The Royal Ballet rehearse Les Sylphides. *Photograph: Johan Persson*
Photograph of Monica Mason on page 4 by Johan Persson

Contents

Welcome from Monica Mason

Welcome to The Royal Ballet Yearbook. In the following pages you can discover more about the distinctive history of our Company, its repertory, dancers and staff, as well as something of what goes on behind the scenes to bring our work to audiences worldwide.

The new Season begins in October with a celebration of Kenneth MacMillan, one of the 20th-century's greatest choreographers who, along with Frederick Ashton, gave The Royal Ballet a unique choreographic heritage. MacMillan would have been 80 this December and so it is appropriate that we open the Season with one of his most powerful full-length works, *Mayerling*. The ballet was made over thirty years ago but the central role remains one of the most challenging ever created for a male dancer.

The second ballet in the Autumn is the Company's signature full-length work, the 19th-century classic *The Sleeping Beauty*. The first new work of the Season, from the Company's Resident Choreographer Wayne McGregor, follows in a mixed programme with George Balanchine's *Agon* and Glen Tetley's *Sphinx*, which enters our repertory for the first time.

In December, for the festive season, Peter Wright's production of *The Nutcracker*, a perennial favourite, is performed alongside a delightful pairing of Ashton's *Les Patineurs* and *Tales of Beatrix Potter*.

Performances of MacMillan's *Romeo and Juliet* start the New Year and continue through February and March. Also in March three of his highly contrasted one-act ballets, *Concerto*, *The Judas Tree* (his last work for The Royal Ballet) and *Elite Syncopations*, can be seen in a programme together. The second world premiere of the Season opens the February–March mixed programme and gives Company dancer Jonathan Watkins his first opportunity to choreograph a work for the main stage. Kim Brandstrup's *Rushes* and McGregor's *Infra*, both recently created for the Company, complete this programme.

Later in the Spring, come two of our Founder Choreographer Frederick Ashton's full-length gems, *La Fille mal gardée* and *Cinderella*.

The final mixed programmes of the Season in April, May and June comprise two works by Christopher Wheeldon, *Tryst* and *Electric Counterpoint*, McGregor's *Chroma*, Mats Ek's *Carmen* and Balanchine's *Symphony in C*. The final new work of the Season is by Liam Scarlett, another of the Company's young dancers who, like Watkins, will be creating on the main stage for the first time.

I hope you enjoy the variety of works that I have selected for the new Season and that you will find much of interest in this companion book.

Monica Mason

Dame Monica Mason DBE
Director, The Royal Ballet

The Company

This page:
Alexandra Ansanelli

Opposite page: As The
Sugar Plum Fairy in *The
Nutcracker*
Photograph: Bill Cooper

Alexandra Ansanelli: Principal 2006–9

Alexandra Ansanelli joined The Royal Ballet from New York
City Ballet in 2006 as First Soloist and was promoted to
Principal in 2007. She retired from dancing at the end of
the 2008/9 Season, when she spoke to Jane Bentham.

**What have been the highlights of working with
The Royal Ballet?**

I'd definitely say dancing the classics – *The Sleeping
Beauty* and *Swan Lake* – and heritage works – *Ondine*
and *A Month in the Country* – both of which are
Company gems. I have enjoyed all of the roles I've
played here so much because they've taught me
something about myself and the Company, and also
about the history of dance. You learn something
about everything and anything you do, especially
when working on signature classics that have been
passed down through so many generations. You can
also appreciate other dancers even more from having
experienced it yourself because you have learnt the
process and can understand what has gone into it.
Knowledge creates more respect, especially for your
predecessors.

**Did you feel a certain amount of responsibility when you
were trusted with Fonteyn's signature role in *Ondine*?**

Well, yes. But life is full of pressure, whatever you do.
I did want to present it properly and Ondine was a
challenge because of not having the background and
education that most of the Company members have,
the classical training or even the Royal Ballet training.
And having started ballet late doesn't help, either. My
whole career I've felt that I've been trying to catch up
with everyone else. With Ondine I was trying to create

a classical image, something that the audience and
Company have envisioned for the role, and also bring
my own interpretation to it. It's finding the balance
between making a role your own in some ways and in
some ways not.
I really did love dancing in *Ondine*. It's one of the
Company's jewels and very meaningful to perform.
It's meaningful on a personal level but also on a bigger
level. When a piece means something important to the
establishment that you are with, it makes it even more
special to dance because you know that it is something
special to the Company.

6

You were widely praised by the dance critics for Ondine. What was it about the role that enabled you to give such a good performance?

Although *Ondine* has a narrative, it is in a sense not as structured as a pure classical work and there is a bit more freedom in it, which I do well in. I like to have that kind of space and room to play with something. And this freedom allows you to bring yourself into it a little more.

Also, *Ondine* has come at a different phase in my career, especially with its second run of the Season, which ended just a few days ago. I felt really relaxed and at peace from having accepted that I'm going to retire, which is a decision that I've been battling with for a while. When your soul is at rest, it enables you to better explore a role and let yourself go.

And what about the other Ashton work you mentioned, *A Month in the Country*?

It's based on a play and you feel like you are on the set of one. The words are the steps, but you are telling the story through the emotional action as well. It's very subtle – that big word – which is something I've had to understand the meaning of in terms of performance. Balanchine's works are very much about making things big and being expansive. For my roles here, I've had to learn to be more relaxed and not to show as much. I joined the Company to learn its style and channel this different energy.

I think the British are very good about small details, which can be so important dramatically. It is a great life-lesson to an artist working on something like *Month*, which is so human: it's the human aspect that makes these works so real and emotive to the people who watch them and also to those who dance them. I've really enjoyed learning these acting roles because they have been such a big change for me from the type of role I danced in New York.

Which other dramatic roles have you performed with the Company?

Not as many as I would have liked because of injury. I missed my debut as Juliet, which was a huge shame. I would have also liked to play Giselle. I knew I needed to change something in my life because I kept on getting sick and becoming injured.

7

But you did make your debut as Odette/Odile in *Swan Lake* this Season.

Yes. That's a dramatic work, but not in the same way as a MacMillan ballet. However, it was always a dream for me to do *Swan Lake* – when you think of ballet, you think of *Swan Lake*. Aurora in *The Sleeping Beauty* was another classical role that I absolutely adored performing. I also loved *La Bayadère* because of the drama, costumes and the character I was dancing: it was fun to play a snob and someone so unlike myself. Technically, it was a very different type of challenge from Balanchine's high-intensity works like *Rubies*, where you have to peak straight away and are only on stage for a short time. In *Bayadère* you have a little more leeway because you have the whole evening to prove yourself.

What will you do next?

I'll be moving back to New York. I don't know at this point what the future holds. I need time to think and re-evaluate, and at the moment I'm just concentrating on finishing on a really high note.

I have never, ever, thought beyond the box as far as what I could do other than dance and retiring has been a very difficult decision to make because I have a great passion for the stage. Since the age of 12, I have committed my whole life to ballet and had a very intense and fast-moving career, and everything in my personal life has taken a back seat. It has been completely worth it but at the same time another part of me needs to keep growing so that I can find a better balance in life. We have only one life to live and there's still a lot I want to do and explore.

What will you miss most about The Royal Ballet?

I'll miss the people. I've enjoyed being around such an interesting group of artists and teachers. It's been extremely insightful in so many ways. I'll also miss being a part of the Royal Opera House. It is an amazing establishment – there are only a few houses of art in the world that combine opera and ballet at such a high level. I think it's really important that art is maintained in this way, and what I have learned here will stay with me forever. I feel proud to have been a part of this great Company and institution.

Alexandra's final performances were *Rubies* on the main stage at Covent Garden on 16 June 2009, and *A Month in the Country* on tour with the Company shortly afterwards. She observes, 'It's kind of ironic: to dance a Balanchine work to say goodbye in England and an Ashton to say goodbye in America' – certainly to tremendous applause from both sides of the Atlantic.

Andrew Hurst, Company Manager

In April 2009, Andrew Hurst joined The Royal Ballet as Company Manager. He is responsible for the efficient running of the Company, acting as liaison and co-ordinator between all the different aspects of its management, including administrative and artistic staff. As he described it, only a matter of weeks into taking up the post, 'The days are all very different, and there is so much to keep track of here. There's quite a lot of movement through this office on a weekly basis – guest artists and teachers, choreographers, conductors, musicians, composers and designers... I am excited by the level of activity in this Company. It's a challenge I look forward to embracing.'

Like many of the staff who run The Royal Ballet, he comes to management from a background in dancing. He trained at The Royal Ballet School – both the Lower and Upper Schools – appearing as a student in the Company's *Swan Lake*, *The Nutcracker*, *Cinderella*, *The Sleeping Beauty* and *The Firebird*. He then worked as a dancer in other companies for 15 years. So, returning now to The Royal Ballet 'is a bit like coming full circle, and it means I can fully appreciate where I am now, what it means, and what a special place this is'.

The Company Manager's role is highly varied and is closely linked to the other three senior management roles in the Company: Director Monica Mason, Associate Director Jeanetta Laurence and Administrative Director Kevin O'Hare (who was the previous Company Manager). Andrew describes his first weekly 'gang of four' meeting: 'I arrived early, and was invited into Monica's office, where I looked around the walls at all the pictures: Ashton, MacMillan, a painting of Monica, the Queen in the Royal box… .' But when Monica realized he was soaking up the environment, she smiled at him and said archly, 'Be careful, she's looking over your shoulder'. Turning round, Andrew discovered that behind him was a picture of the founder of the Company, Dame Ninette de Valois.

Does he miss being a dancer? 'Not yet! I have been taking steps toward this kind of role for quite a while: I studied Business and Management and gained managerial experience in other companies while dancing at the same time.' A dancer until 2008, Andrew's experience of company management began while he was still with Rambert Dance Company, where he led the newly formed Dancers' Management Team. Following the departure of the company's General Manager, Andrew took over the project management of special events and foreign touring. Then he became General Manager for Phoenix Dance Theatre in Leeds, 'a tiny company in comparison' but which gave him the necessary experience to run a dance company. 'We only had a part-time accountant, for example, and so I was doing a lot of financial work on top of my everyday jobs. It's nice not to have that additional responsibility here. At The Royal Ballet there is a large group of people, all with clearly defined roles, but who work together as a team: this has been a big change for me. I don't feel so much on my own. In addition, there were 10 dancers in Phoenix and 22 in Rambert compared to the 96 we have here.'

Andrew has a life-long love of languages and is fluent in several, partly as a result of his international dancing career. He joined Basel Ballet in Switzerland and appeared as a guest with its sister companies, Ballett der Städtischen Bühnen in Dortmund and Ballett der Oper der Stadt in Bonn. Then he joined Ballet Gulbenkian in Portugal before moving to Netherlands Dans Theater 2. Following this he was a guest soloist with Berlin Ballet Komische Oper before returning to the UK to Rambert in 2000. A skill with languages is a very practical bonus in such an international Company as The Royal Ballet. 'The Company has many international dancers and it's sometimes important to

chat in their own language, or just to appreciate how international their work is.'

On the business side too, Andrew's linguistic knowledge has proved of immediate practical help. 'One of them in particular, Spanish, is coming in quite handy at the moment', he explained amid plans for the Summer 2009 Company tour to Cuba, Spain and Washington D.C. 'We visited Cuba a couple of weeks ago to sort out the contracts and there none of them were expecting an Englishman to speak Spanish so fluently, which made dealing with them much easier. It's an advantage to be able to use a language in that way.'

Co-ordinating The Royal Ballet tour each year is a Herculean task, since it involves almost all the dancers and staff of the Company as they move between three, four and sometimes more destinations. 'I've had quite a lot of help for my first year: Kevin has put everything in place more or less, and the Deputy Company Manager Elizabeth Ferguson has been a huge support. I'm quite surprised by how many changes there are, even right up to the last minute before we leave.'

For this tour and future ones, he hopes to build on his experience of touring to Europe, Russia, China and all over Eastern Europe with Rambert, and to South Africa, North and South America, Australia and Singapore with other companies. 'The biggest difference for me now is the scale of it, with nearly 150 people travelling! We fly first to Washington D.C., then return to London for a few days, next on to Granada for two performances and then Cuba. I will accompany the first group to leave London and hopefully, by the time we all arrive in Washington, the containers with all the costumes, shoes and equipment will already be there!

'Ultimately, it seems to me the role of the Company Manager needs to combine the administrative and logistical aspects of the Company with a sympathy for the needs of the dancers,' Andrew concludes. And with his varied career both on the stage as a dancer and behind the scenes, managing both the everyday concerns and those last-minute surprises, Andrew is well-placed for the rewarding challenge of keeping in fine order the machinery that keeps The Royal Ballet dancing.

During the 2008/9 Season

Ruth Bailey joined the Company from The Royal Ballet School as Artist and **Jacqueline Clark** (ex Royal Ballet School) joined from Ballet Ireland as Artist.

First Soloist **Isabel McMeekan** and First Artist **Henry St Clair** left the Company.

Anthony Russell Roberts retired as Administrative Director of the Company, succeeded by **Kevin O'Hare**, and **Andrew Hurst** succeeded Kevin as Company Manager. **Jeanetta Laurence** was promoted to Associate Director of the Company. **Janine Limberg** retired as Head of Press, succeeded by **Rosie Neave**, and Press Assistant **Faye Turner** left the Administrative Staff.

At the end of the Season, Principal **Alexandra Ansanelli** and Soloist and Assistant Ballet Mistress **Vanessa Palmer** left the Company.

For the 2009/10 Season

First Soloist **Steven McRae** is promoted to Principal. Soloists **Helen Crawford**, **Hikaru Kobayashi** and **Sergei Polunin** are promoted to First Soloist.

First Artist **Kristen McNally** is promoted to Soloist. Artists **Leanne Cope**, **Olivia Cowley**, **Melissa Hamilton** and **Nathalie Harrison** are promoted to First Artist.

Tristan Dyer, **Benjamin Ella** and **Leticia Stock** join the Company from The Royal Ballet School as Artists. **Hayley Forskitt** (ex Royal Ballet School) joins the Company from Norwegian National Ballet as Artist, and Prix de Lausanne Dancer **Akane Takada** joins the Company as Artist. **Rina Nemoto** joins the Company as Prix de Lausanne Dancer.

Sian Murphy becomes Assistant Ballet Mistress while continuing to dance as First Artist and **Vanessa Palmer** will appear as Guest Principal Character Artist.

Artistic and Administrative Staff 2008/9

Artistic Staff
Back Row *Left to right,* Grant Coyle, Lesley Collier, Jonathan Cope, Christopher Carr, Gary Avis, Christopher Saunders, Philip Mosley, Alexander Agadzhanov.
Front Row *(seated),* *Left to right,* David Pickering, Jeanetta Laurence, Mayumi Hotta, Ursula Hageli and Vanessa Palmer.
Staff also includes: Anna Trevien, Elizabeth Anderton, Clare Thurman.
Photograph: Rob Moore

Administration
Back Row *Left to right,* Heather Baxter, Kevin O'Hare, Yvonne Hunte, Janine Limberg, Anthony Russell-Roberts, Orsola Ricciardelli, Elizabeth Ferguson, Gavin Fitzpatrick.
Front Row *(seated)* *Left to right,* Hayley Smith and Faye Turner.
Staff also includes: Andrew Hurst and Rosie Neave.
Photograph: Rob Moore

The Company

Music Staff, Physiotherapy and Body Control Instructors, and Stage Management 2008/9

Music Staff
Left to right, Robert Clark, Jonathan Beavis, Philip Cornfield, Paul Stobart, Kate Shipway, Barry Wordsworth, Henry Roche, Tim Qualtrough
Photograph: Rob Moore

Stage Management
Left to right, Lucy Summers, Lynne Otto, Johanna Adams
Photograph: Rob Moore

Physiotherapy and Body Control Instructors
Left to right, Moira McCormack, Daryl Martin, Fiona Kleckham, Jane Paris. Staff also includes: Helen Wellington, Konrad Simpson, Britt Tajet-Foxell, Tatina Semprini.
Photograph: Rob Moore

13

Principal Guest Artists and Principals 2009/10

PRINCIPAL GUEST ARTISTS

Carlos Acosta
Joined as Principal 1998, Principal
Guest Artist 2003
Born: Havana, Cuba
Trained: National Ballet School
of Cuba
Previous Companies: English
National Ballet (1991), National Ballet
of Cuba (1992), Houston Ballet (1993)

Miyako Yoshida
Joined as Principal 1995, Principal
Guest Artist 2008
Born: Tokyo, Japan
Trained: Tokyo, The Royal Ballet
School
Previous Companies: Sadler's Wells
Royal Ballet / Birmingham Royal
Ballet (1984)

PRINCIPALS

Leanne Benjamin
Joined 1992, promoted to Principal
1993
Born: Rockhampton, Australia
Trained: The Royal Ballet School

Federico Bonelli
Joined as Principal 2003
Born: Genoa, Italy
Trained: Turin Dance Academy
Previous Companies: Zurich Ballet
(1996), Dutch National Ballet (1999)

Alina Cojocaru
Joined 1999, promoted to Principal
2001
Born: Bucharest, Romania
Trained: Kiev Ballet School,
The Royal Ballet School
Previous Company: Kiev Ballet
(1998)

Lauren Cuthbertson
Joined 2002, promoted to Principal
2008
Born: Devon, England
Trained: The Royal Ballet School

Mara Galeazzi
Joined 1992, promoted to Principal
2003
Born: Brescia, Italy
Trained: La Scala Ballet School,
Milan

Johan Kobborg
Joined as Principal 1999
Born: Odense, Denmark
Trained: Royal Danish Ballet School
Previous Company: Royal Danish
Ballet (1991)

Sarah Lamb
Joined 2004, promoted to Principal
2006
Born: Boston, USA
Trained: Boston Ballet School
Previous Company: Boston Ballet
(1998)

David Makhateli
Joined 2003, promoted to Principal
2008
Born: Tbilisi, Georgia
Trained: The Royal Ballet School

14

The Company

Steven McRae
Joined 2004, promoted to Principal
2009
Born: Sydney, Australia
Trained: The Royal Ballet School

Roberta Marquez
Joined and promoted to Principal
2004
Born: Rio de Janeiro, Brazil
Trained: Maria Olenewa State Dance
School
Previous Company: Municipal
Theatre Ballet, Rio de Janeiro (1994)

Laura Morera
Joined 1995, promoted to Principal
2007
Born: Madrid, Spain
Trained: The Royal Ballet School

Marianela Nuñez
Joined 1998, promoted to Principal
2002
Born: Buenos Aires
Trained: Teatro Colón Ballet School,
The Royal Ballet School

Rupert Pennefather
Joined 1999, promoted to Principal
2008
Born: Maidenhead, England
Trained: The Royal Ballet School

Ivan Putrov
Joined 1998, promoted to Principal
2002
Born: Kiev, Ukraine
Trained: Kiev State Choreographic
Institute, The Royal Ballet School

Tamara Rojo
Joined as Principal 1999
Born: Montreal, Canada
Trained: Victor Ullate Ballet School,
Madrid
Previous Companies: Victor Ullate
Ballet (1991), Scottish Ballet (1996),
English National Ballet (1997)

Viacheslav Samodurov
Joined and promoted to Principal
2003
Born: Tallinn, Estonia
Trained: Vaganova Ballet Academy
Previous Companies: Mariinsky
Ballet (1992), Dutch National Ballet
(2000)

Thiago Soares
Joined 2002, promoted to Principal
2006
Born: São Gonçalo, Brazil
Trained: Centre for Dance, Rio de
Janeiro
Previous Company: Rio de Janeiro
Municipal Theatre Ballet (1998)

Edward Watson
Joined 1994, promoted to Principal
2005
Born: Bromley, England
Trained: The Royal Ballet School

Zenaida Yanowsky
Joined 1994, promoted to Principal
2001
Born: Lyon, France
Trained: Las Palmas, Majorca
Previous Company: Paris Opéra
Ballet (1994)

**PRINCIPAL
CHARACTER ARTISTS**
Left to right
**Gary Avis
Elizabeth McGorian
Alastair Marriott
Genesia Rosato**

Christopher Saunders

**CHARACTER ARTIST
Philip Mosley**

FIRST SOLOISTS
Left to right
**Ricardo Cervera
Deirdre Chapman
Yuhui Choe
Helen Crawford**

**Bennet Gartside
Valeri Hristov
Hikaru Kobayashi
José Martín**

Sergei Polunin
Yohei Sasaki

SOLOISTS
Left to right
Christina Arestis
Victoria Hewitt

Ryoichi Hirano
Jonathan Howells
Paul Kay
Bethany Keating

Kenta Kura
Iohna Loots
Laura McCulloch
Kristen McNally

Brian Maloney
David Pickering
Samantha Raine
Johannes Stepanek

Soloists,
First Artists and Artists
2009/10

Gemma Sykes
Eric Underwood
Thomas Whitehead

FIRST ARTISTS
Left to right
Tara-Brigitte Bhavnani
Leanne Cope
Olivia Cowley
Vanessa Fenton

Francesca Filpi
Melissa Hamilton
Nathalie Harrison
Elizabeth Harrod

Cindy Jourdain
Emma Maguire
Ernst Meisner
Pietra Mello-Pittman

18

Sian Murphy
Ludovic Ondiviela
Romany Pajdak
Richard Ramsey

Liam Scarlett
Michael Stojko
Lara Turk
Andrej Uspenski

Jonathan Watkins
James Wilkie

ARTISTS
Left to right
Ruth Bailey
Claire Calvert
Jacqueline Clark
Celisa Diuana

Artists 2009/10

Tristan Dyer
Benjamin Ella
Kevin Emerton
Hayley Forskitt

Elsa Godard
James Hay
Fernando Montaño
Erico Montes

Demelza Parish
Xander Parish
Gemma Pitchley-Gale
Leticia Stock

Akane Takada
Dawid Trzensimiech
Sabina Westcombe

PRIX DE LAUSANNE
DANCER
Rina Nemoto

20

The Royal Ballet 2009/10

Patron HM The Queen
President HRH The Prince of Wales
Vice-President The Lady Sarah Chatto

Director Dame Monica Mason DBE
Associate Director Jeanetta Laurence
Administrative Director Kevin O'Hare

Music Director Barry Wordsworth
Resident Choreographer
 Wayne McGregor

Company Manager
Andrew Hurst

Financial Controller
Heather Baxter

**Artistic Administrator
and Character Artist**
Philip Mosley

Contracts Administrator
Hayley Smith

**Deputy Company
Manager**
Elizabeth Ferguson

**Administrative
Co-ordinator**
Yvonne Hunte

**Management
Accountant**
Orsola Ricciardelli

**Artistic Administrative
Assistant**
Gavin Fitzpatrick

Education Manager
Clare Thurman

**Artistic and Education
Co-ordinator**
David Pickering

**Head of Physiotherapy
and Chartered
Physiotherapist**
Moira McCormack

**Chartered
Physiotherapist**
Daryl Martin

**Body Control
Instructors**
Jane Paris
Fiona Kleckham

**Occupational
Psychologist**
Britt Tajet-Foxell

Masseurs
Tatina Semprini
Konrad Simpson
Helen Wellington

**Consultant Orthopaedic
Surgeon**
Lloyd Williams

Medical Advisor
Ian Beasley

Ballet Master
Christopher Saunders

Ballet Mistress
Ursula Hageli

Assistant Ballet Master
Gary Avis

Assistant Ballet Mistress
Sian Murphy

**Senior Teacher and
Répétiteur to the
Principal Artists**
Alexander Agadzhanov

Répétiteurs
Lesley Collier
Jonathan Cope

**Principal Dance Notator
and Répétiteur**
Grant Coyle

Dance Notators
Mayumi Hotta
Anna Trevien

Head of Music Staff
Henry Roche

Music Staff
Jonathan Beavis
Philip Cornfield
Robert Clark
Tim Qualtrough
Kate Shipway
Paul Stobart

**Guest Principal
Ballet Master**
Christopher Carr

Principal Guest Teacher
Elizabeth Anderton

Guest Teachers
Loipa Araujo
Johnny Eliasen
Olga Evreinoff
David Howard
Roland Price
Violette Verdy

Conductors
Daniel Capps
Dominic Grier*
Boris Gruzin
Koen Kessels
James MacMillan
Paul Murphy
Valeriy Ovsyanikov
Pavel Sorokin
Barry Wordsworth
Martin Yates

Principals
Carlos Acosta†
Leanne Benjamin
Roberto Bolle††
Federico Bonelli
Alina Cojocaru
Lauren Cuthbertson
Mara Galeazzi
Johan Kobborg
Sarah Lamb
David Makhateli
Steven McRae
Roberta Marquez
Laura Morera
Marianela Nuñez
Rupert Pennefather
Ivan Putrov
Tamara Rojo
Viacheslav Samodurov
Thiago Soares
Edward Watson
Zenaida Yanowsky
Miyako Yoshida†

**Principal Character
Artists**
Gary Avis
David Drew††
Elizabeth McGorian
Alastair Marriott
Vanessa Palmer††
Gillian Revie††
Genesia Rosato
Christopher Saunders
William Tuckett††

First Soloists
Ricardo Cervera
Deirdre Chapman
Yuhui Choe
Helen Crawford
Bennet Gartside
Valeri Hristov
Hikaru Kobayashi
José Martín
Sergei Polunin
Yohei Sasaki

Soloists
Christina Arestis
Victoria Hewitt
Ryoichi Hirano
Jonathan Howells
Paul Kay
Bethany Keating
Kenta Kura
Iohna Loots
Laura McCulloch
Kristen McNally
Brian Maloney
David Pickering
Samantha Raine
Johannes Stepanek
Gemma Sykes
Eric Underwood
Thomas Whitehead

First Artists
Tara-Brigitte Bhavnani
Leanne Cope
Olivia Cowley
Vanessa Fenton
Francesca Filpi
Melissa Hamilton
Nathalie Harrison
Elizabeth Harrod
Cindy Jourdain
Emma Maguire
Ernst Meisner
Pietra Mello-Pittman
Sian Murphy
Ludovic Ondiviela
Romany Pajdak
Richard Ramsey
Liam Scarlett
Michael Stojko
Lara Turk
Andrej Uspenski
Jonathan Watkins
James Wilkie

Artists
Ruth Bailey
Claire Calvert
Jacqueline Clark
Celisa Diuana
Tristan Dyer
Benjamin Ella
Kevin Emerton
Hayley Forskitt
Elsa Godard
James Hay
Fernando Montaño
Erico Montes
Demelza Parish
Xander Parish
Gemma Pitchley-Gale
Leticia Stock
Akane Takada
Dawid Trzensimiech
Sabina Westcombe

**Prix de Lausanne
Dancer**
Rina Nemoto

* Jette Parker
  Young Artist
† Principal Guest Artist
†† Guest Artist

Season Images
Looking Back at 2008/9

Swan Lake
Ballet in four acts

Music
Pyotr Il'yich Tchaikovsky
Choreography
Marius Petipa
and Lev Ivanov
Additional Choreography
Frederick Ashton
(Act III Neapolitan Dance)
and David Bintley
(Act I Waltz)

Production
Anthony Dowell
Designs
Yolanda Sonnabend
Lighting design
Mark Henderson
Staging
Christopher Carr
Ballet Mistress
Ursula Hageli
Principal Coaching
Alexander Agadzhanov,
Lesley Collier, Jonathan
Cope, Roland Price
Notators
Grant Coyle,
Anna Trevien

Premieres: 27 January
1895 (Mariinsky Theatre,
St Petersburg); 12 March
1987 (The Royal Ballet,
this production)

**Swan Lake
(October, March)**
This page: Alexandra
Ansanelli as Odette
and David Makhateli
as Prince Siegfried
Opposite page: the
Corps de Ballet
Photographs:
Dee Conway

22

23

Manon
Ballet in three acts

Music
Jules Massenet
*Orchestrated
and arranged by*
Leighton Lucas *with
the collaboration of*
Hilda Gaunt
Choreography
Kenneth MacMillan

Designs
Nicholas Georgiadis
Lighting design
John B. Read
Staging
Monica Mason
and Monica Parker
Ballet Master
Christopher Saunders
Ballet Mistress
Ursula Hageli
Principal Coaching
Alexander Agadzhanov,
Lesley Collier, Jonathan
Cope, Monica Mason,
Monica Parker

Premiere: 7 March 1974
(The Royal Ballet)

**Manon
(October –
November)**

This page, top:
Roberta Marquez
as Manon and Ivan
Putrov as Des Grieux

Bottom left: Laura
Morera as Lescaut's
Mistress

Bottom right:
Tamara Rojo
as Manon

Opposite page:
The Corps de Ballet

Photographs:
Bill Cooper

24

25

Serenade

Music
Pyotr Il'yich Tchaikovsky

Choreography
George Balanchine

Costume designs
Barbara Karinska
Lighting design
John B. Read
Staging
Patricia Neary
Ballet Master
Christopher Saunders
Notator
Anna Trevien

Premieres: 1 March 1935
(School of American
Ballet, American Ballet at
Adelphi Theatre); 7 May
1964 (The Royal Ballet)

Mixed Programme
(October –
November)

This page, left:
Marianela Nuñez and
Rupert Pennefather
in *Serenade*

Right: Mara Galeazzi
in *Serenade*

*Opposite page, top
left:* Federico Bonelli
in *L'Invitation au
voyage*

Top right: Marianela
Nuñez and Sergei
Polunin in *L'Invitation
au voyage*

Bottom: Johan
Kobborg and Artists
of The Royal Ballet in
Theme and Variations

Photographs:
Johan Persson

26

L'Invitation au voyage

L'Invitation au voyage is dedicated to Beryl Margaret Coleman, my mother. (Michael Corder, 16 March 1982)

Music
Henri Duparc
Choreography
Michael Corder

Designs
Yolanda Sonnabend
Lighting design
Paul Pyant
Staging
Michael Corder
Ballet Master
Jonathan Cope
Notator and Assistant to the Choreographer
Diana Curry

Premiere: 16 March 1982 (The Royal Ballet)

Theme and Variations

Music
Pyotr Il'yich Tchaikovsky
Choreography
George Balanchine

Designs
Peter Farmer
Lighting design
John B. Read
Staging
Patricia Neary
Ballet Master
Christopher Saunders
Ballet Mistress
Ursula Hageli

Premieres: 26 November 1947 (Ballet Theatre); 5 March 2007 (The Royal Ballet)

Voluntaries

Music
Francis Poulenc
Choreography
Glen Tetley

Designs
Rouben Ter-Arutunian
Lighting design
John B. Read
Staging
Bronwen Curry
Ballet Mistress
Ursula Hageli
Principal Coaching
Lesley Collier

Premieres: 22 December
1973 (Stuttgart Ballet);
18 November 1976
(The Royal Ballet)

**Mixed Programme
(November)**

This page: Sergei
Polunin in *Voluntaries*

Opposite page: Yuhui
Choe as the Pupil
and Edward Watson
as the Teacher in
The Lesson

Photographs:
Bill Cooper

28

The Lesson

Music
Georges Delerue
Choreography
Flemming Flindt *based
on the play by*
Eugene Ionesco

Set designs
Flemming Flindt
after Bernard Daydé
Costume designs
Flemming Flindt
and Tina Sander
Lighting design
Simon Bennison
Ballet Mistress
Ursula Hageli

Premieres: 6 April 1964
(Paris Opéra Comique);
6 October 2005
(The Royal Ballet)

29

Infra

Infra is dedicated to
Dame Monica Mason DBE
in celebration of her
50th Season with
The Royal Ballet

Music
Max Richter

Choreography
Wayne McGregor

Set designs
Julian Opie

Costume designs
Moritz Junge

Lighting design
Lucy Carter

Sound design
Chris Ekers

Assistant Ballet Mistress
Vanessa Palmer

Notator
Darren Parish

Premiere: 13 November
2008 (The Royal Ballet)

**Mixed Programme
(November)**

This page: Dancers
of The Royal Ballet
in *Infra*

Opposite page:
Edward Watson
in *Infra*

Photographs:
Bill Cooper

30

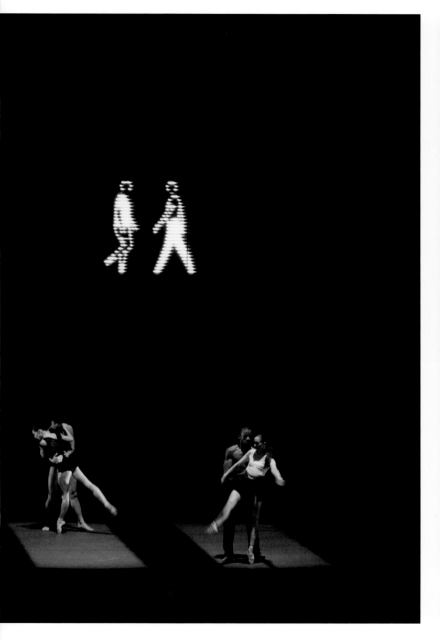

31

Ondine
Ballet in three acts

Music
Hans Werner Henze
Choreography
Frederick Ashton

Designs
Lila de Nobili
Lighting design
John B. Read
Staging
Christopher Carr,
Grant Coyle
Principal Coaching
Alexander Agadzhanov,
Jonathan Cope,
Grant Coyle

Premiere: 27 October
1958 (The Royal Ballet)

**Ondine
(November –
December)**
This page (left):
Miyako Yoshida
as Ondine
Photograph:
Bill Cooper

Right: Alexandra
Ansanelli as Ondine
Photograph:
Dee Conway

**The Nutcracker
(December –
January)**
Opposite page:
Steven McRae as
the Prince
Photograph:
Johan Persson

32

The Nutcracker
Ballet in two acts

Music
Pyotr Il'yich Tchaikovsky
Choreography
Peter Wright
after Lev Ivanov
Original scenario
Marius Petipa
after E.T.A. Hoffmann's
*Nussknacker und
Mausekönig*

Production and scenario
Peter Wright
Designs
Julia Trevelyan Oman
Lighting design
Mark Henderson
Production Consultant
Roland John Wiley
Staging
Christopher Carr
Ballet Mistress
Ursula Hageli
Principal Coaching
Alexander Agadzhanov,
Lesley Collier,
Jonathan Cope,
Roland Price,
Christopher Saunders
Dance Notators
Grant Coyle,
Anna Trevien

Premieres: 18 December
1892 (Mariinsky
Theatre, St Petersburg);
20 December 1984
(The Royal Ballet, this
production); 17 December
1999 (revisions to this
production)

33

La Bayadère
Ballet in three acts

Music
Ludwig Minkus
orchestrated by
John Lanchbery
Choreography
Natalia Makarova *after*
Marius Petipa
Production conceived
and directed by
Natalia Makarova

Set designs
Pier Luigi Samaritani
Costume designs
Yolanda Sonnabend
Lighting design
John B. Read
Revival staging
Olga Evreinoff

Premieres: 4 February
1877 (Imperial Bolshoi
Kamenny Theatre,
St Petersburg); 18 May
1989 (The Royal Ballet,
this production)

La Bayadère
(January – February)

This page: Marianela
Nuñez as Gamzatti

Opposite page:
Sergei Polunin as
Solor

Photographs:
Bill Cooper

35

The Seven Deadly Sins
Ballet chanté in
nine scenes

Music Kurt Weill
Text Bertolt Brecht
Low voice arrangement
Wilhelm Brückner-Rüggeberg
English translation
W.H. Auden
and Chester Kallman
Choreography
Will Tuckett
*Assistant to the
Choreographer*
Pia Furtado

Designs
Lez Brotherston
Lighting design
Paule Constable
Video Designs
Leo Warner and Mark
Grimmer for Fifty Nine
Productions Limited
Sound design
Andrew Bruce
Dance Notator
Anna Trevien

Premiere: 26 April 2007
(The Royal Ballet)

**Mixed Programme
(February)**
Right: Thiago
Soares as strip
club owner and
Zenaida Yanowsky as
Anna II in *The Seven
Deadly Sins*
Photograph:
Bill Cooper

36

Carmen

Music
Georges Bizet *arranged by* Rodion Shchedrin
Choreography
Mats Ek

Designs
Marie-Louise Ekman
Designer's Assistant
Peder Freiij
Lighting design
Jürgen Jansson
Staging
Pompea Santoro and Veli-Pekka Peltokallio
Dance Notator
Mayumi Hotta

Premieres: 13 May 1992 (Cullberg Ballet); 10 April 2002 (The Royal Ballet)

Mixed Programme (February)

Left (top): Tamara Rojo as Carmen and Bennet Gartside as Escamillo in *Carmen*

Bottom: Andrej Uspenski, José Martín, Ryoichi Hirano and Ernst Meisner in *Carmen*

Photographs: Dee Conway

37

DGV: Danse à grande vitesse

Music
Michael Nyman

Choreography
Christopher Wheeldon

Designs
Jean-Marc Puissant

Lighting design
Jennifer Tipton

Ballet Master
Christopher Saunders

Dance Notator
Anna Trevien

Premiere: 17 November
2006 (The Royal Ballet)

**Mixed Programme
(February)**

This page: Marianela
Nuñez and Federico
Bonelli in *DGV: Danse
à grande vitesse*

Opposite page:
Leanne Benjamin and
Edward Watson in
*DGV: Danse à grande
vitesse*

Photographs:
Johan Persson

38

39

Royal Ballet
Yearbook 2009/10

Isadora

Deborah MacMillan would like to dedicate *Isadora* to the memory of Norman Morrice, who shared Kenneth's belief in the infinite possibilities of dance.

Music
Richard Rodney Bennett

Additional orchestrations
Martin Ward

Choreography
Kenneth MacMillan

Production and setting
Deborah MacMillan

Costume and prop designs
Barry Kay

Lighting design
John B. Read

Sound design
Andrew Bruce

Film direction
Lynne Wake

Film editing
Christopher Bird

Staging
Julie Lincoln

Ballet Mistress
Ursula Hageli

Principal Coaching
Jonathan Cope

Dance Notator
Karl Burnett

Premieres: 30 April 1981 (The Royal Ballet); 11 March 2009 (The Royal Ballet, this production)

Mixed Programme (March – April)

Top: Tamara Rojo as Isadora and Edward Watson as Edward Gordon Craig in *Isadora*

Bottom: Tamara Rojo as Isadora

Photographs: Dee Conway

40

Dances at a Gathering

Music
Fryderyk Chopin

Choreography
Jerome Robbins

Costume designs
Joe Eula
Lighting design
Jennifer Tipton
Staging
Susan Hendl, Ben Huys
Ballet Master
Christopher Saunders
Notator
Mayumi Hotta

Premieres: 22 May 1969
(The New York City
Ballet, State Theatre,
New York); 19 Ocober
1970 (The Royal Ballet)

Mixed Programme
(March – April)

Top: Lauren
Cuthbertson as
Mauve and Edward
Watson as Green
in *Dances at a
Gathering*
Bottom: Laura
Morera as Apricot
in *Dances at a
Gathering*
Photographs:
Dee Conway

41

Dido and Aeneas
(with The Royal Opera)
Opera in three acts

Music
Henry Purcell
Libretto
Nahum Tate

*Director and
Choreographer*
Wayne McGregor
*Assistant Director and
Assistant Choreographer*
Laïla Diallo
Set designs
Hildegard Bechtler
Costume designs
Fotini Dimou
Lighting design
Lucy Carter
Projection design
Mark Hatchard for
HotBox Studios

Premieres: December
1689; 26 June 2006
(La Scala, Milan,
this production)

This page: Liam
Scarlett and Brian
Maloney in *Dido
and Aeneas*

Opposite page (left):
Edward Watson as
Acis with Danielle
de Niese (soprano)
as Galatea; *(right)*
Melissa Hamilton and
Steven McRae as
Damon in *Acis and
Galatea*

Photographs:
Bill Cooper

42

Acis and Galatea
(with The Royal Opera)
Pastoral opera in
two acts

Music
George Frideric Handel
Libretto
John Gay, Alexander
Pope and John Hughes

Director and
Choreographer
Wayne McGregor
Assistant Director and
Assistant Choreographer
Laïla Diallo
Designs
Hildegard Bechtler
Lighting design
Lucy Carter

Premieres: Summer 1718;
10 June 1732 (revised
version); 31 March 2009
(The Royal Opera,
The Royal Ballet,
this production)

Giselle
Ballet in two acts

Music
Adolphe Adam *revised by* Joseph Horovitz
Scenario
Théophile Gautier
after Heinrich Heine

Production
Peter Wright
Designs
John Macfarlane
Original lighting design
Jennifer Tipton
Re-created by
Clare O'Donoghue
Staging
Christopher Carr
Ballet Mistress
Ursula Hageli
Principal Coaching
Alexander Agadzhanov,
Jonathan Cope, Lesley
Collier, Donald MacLeary,
Monica Mason, Vanessa
Palmer, Roland Price
Dance Notator
Grant Coyle

Premieres: 28 June
1841 (Paris: original
choreography by Jean
Coralli and Jules Perrot;
later revisions by
Petipa, notably 1884);
28 November 1985
(The Royal Ballet, this
production)

Giselle (April – May)
Right: Lauren
Cuthbertson as
Giselle and Rupert
Pennefather as
Count Albrecht
Photograph:
Johan Persson

44

The Firebird

Music
Igor Stravinsky

Choreography
Mikhail Fokine

Designs
Natalia Gontcharova

Lighting design
John B. Read

Original staging
Sergey Grigoriev
and Lubov Tchernicheva

Staging
Christopher Carr

Ballet Mistress
Ursula Hageli

Principal Coaching
Jonathan Cope,
Monica Mason

Notator
Grant Coyle

Premieres: 25 June
1910 (Ballet Russes de
Serge Diaghilev, Paris);
23 August 1954 (Sadler's
Wells Ballet, Edinburgh
Festival, this production)

**Mixed Programme
(May)**

Left: Christina
Arestis as the
Beautiful Tsarevna
in *The Firebird*

Right: Roberta
Marquez as the
Firebird and
Valeri Hristov as
Ivan Tsarevich
in *The Firebird*

Photographs:
Johan Persson

45

Les Sylphides

Music
Fryderyk Chopin
Choreography
Mikhail Fokine

Production
Monica Mason
Designs
Alexandre Benois
realized by Suzanne
Hickinbotham
Lighting design
John B. Read
Ballet Mistress
Ursula Hageli
Principal Coaching
Lesley Collier, Jonathan
Cope, Monica Mason
Notator
Anna Trevien

Premieres: 23 February
1907 (Mariinsky Theatre,
St Petersburg); 27 June
1911 (Ballet Russes de
Serge Diaghilev, Paris,
this production); 8 March
1932 (Vic Wells Ballet at
Sadler's Wells Theatre)

**Mixed Programme
(May)**

This page: Johan
Kobborg and
Yuhui Choe in
Les Sylphides

Opposite page:
Lauren Cuthbertson
in *Les Sylphides*

Photographs:
Johan Persson

46

Royal Ballet
Yearbook 2009/10

Sensorium

Music
Claude Debussy
orchestrated by
Colin Matthews
Choreography
Alastair Marriott
*Assistant to the
Choreographer*
Jonathan Howells

Designs
Adam Wiltshire
Lighting design
John B. Read
Notator
Anna Trevien

Premiere: 4 May 2009
(The Royal Ballet)

**Mixed Programme
(May)**
This page (top):
Alexandra Ansanelli
and Rupert
Pennefather; *bottom*
Dancers of The Royal
Ballet in *Sensorium*

Opposite page (top):
Leanne Benjamin and
Thomas Whitehead;
bottom: Rupert
Pennefather in
Sensorium

Photographs:
Johan Persson

48

Jewels
Ballet in three parts

Music
Gabriel Fauré (*Emeralds*),
Igor Stravinsky (*Rubies*),
Pyotr Il'yich Tchaikovsky
(*Diamonds*)
Choreography
George Balanchine

Set designs
Jean-Marc Puissant
Costume designs
Barbara Karinska
*Costume designs
consultant*
Holly Hynes
Lighting design
Jennifer Tipton
Staging
Elyse Borne,
Patricia Neary

Premieres: 13 April
1967 (New York City
Ballet); 23 November
2007 (The Royal Ballet,
this production)

**Jewels
(June)**

This page: **Deirdre
Chapman, Laura
Morera and Steven
McRae in** *Emeralds*

Opposite page: **Laura
McCulloch, Kenta
Kura, Yohei Sasaki,
Bennet Gartside,
Johannes Stepanek
in** *Rubies*

**Photographs:
Bill Cooper**

50

Living the Dream

by Will Richmond

A young dancer may dream of becoming a princess or a prince, a snowflake or a swan; they may dream of applause, of the lights in the theatre, the curtain calls... But most of all they dream that this will be their career. The prospect of becoming a professional dancer is exciting and daunting, for the world of ballet is extraordinarily competitive. For those who succeed in becoming a member of The Royal Ballet or one of the other few leading ballet companies in the world, the transition from student to professional dancer can be difficult, exhilarating and quite simply a dream come true.

Every dancer has their own dreams and aspirations, and every ballet company has their own unique way of doing things. Unlike many companies, The Royal Ballet has a permanent home. The Royal Opera House is probably the busiest opera house in the world, with over 300 performances given each year on the main stage alone. One of the defining aspects of The Royal Ballet as a company, and one of the first things a new dancer notices when they join, is the sheer scope of the repertory. With at least 12 ballet productions in each Season – some of them full-length works, some mixed programmes – The Royal Ballet gives a minimum of 135 performances on the main stage every year. And then there are even more performances in the other theatres in the building, including Draft Works in the Clore Studio Upstairs, and New Works in the Linbury Studio Theatre, where Royal Ballet dancers are given the chance to choreograph works for their fellow dancers. Then there is the tour at the end of each Season which brings more performances to stages overseas.

With so much going on, the schedule of rehearsals and performances for the dancers is hectic and demanding to say the least and a new dancer has to adapt quickly. The dancers begin class at 10.30am, often after having squeezed in their all-important gym or pilates sessions beforehand, and class is followed by back-to-back rehearsals that end with a performance usually at least every other night during the Season. The pace can take some getting used to. Royal Ballet Soloist Eric Underwood, who joined the Company in 2006 from American Ballet Theatre in New York, explains:

> When you join The Royal Ballet you build a different relationship with everything – with dancing, with the works, with your body. At ABT you do rehearsal

52

periods and then performance periods – maybe three weeks at City Centre, maybe ten weeks at the Met – whereas here we rehearse throughout the day and perform in the evenings. We're always going, and your body has to adjust to that, as well as your frame of mind.

Getting to grips with the physical and mental demands of life in The Royal Ballet is essential if the Company is to present one of the most varied and appealing programmes in the world. The Company continues to create eclectic Seasons which include new commissions – both from established choreographers and young choreographers on the rise – as well as the classical works that have been the Company's trademark for decades. Such a variety of roles to perform in quick succession throughout the Season can be exhausting for a dancer, but it is not all suffering in the name of art. 'Sure, physically it's a lot more demanding because you're consistently working,' says Eric, 'but at the same time it can be a lot more rewarding because you get to see yourself in many different lights as a dancer.'

Nonetheless the dancers certainly seem to take it in their stride, and the level of excellence expected of them is crucial to maintaining the degree of perfection experienced by the audience. During one quite normal week this year, for example, the dancers were performing Ashton's *Ondine* every night while rehearsing Balanchine's *Jewels* in the daytime, and also starting rehearsals for the ballets they would take on tour, which ranged from Wayne McGregor's *Chroma* to MacMillan's *Manon*. Rather than finding this a dizzying array of styles, Eric, like many of the dancers, finds this a cause for confidence:

When you're on stage here the thing that is supporting you the most is the structure of

Left: Eric Underwood in rehearsal for Christopher Wheeldon's *Electric Counterpoint*.
Photograph: Johan Persson

rehearsals and stage calls. It's extremely rare not to know exactly what you're doing. You're really well rehearsed, and you've been well briefed on the role that you're trying to convey, and who the character is. There is a great deal of tradition, and everything does have a meaning, so there is so much to draw upon when you're out there on the stage.

Eric came from an already professional background, but for many of the corps de ballet joining The Royal Ballet is their first experience of dancing for a living. Yuhui Choe

53

joined as an Artist in 2003 after a year's apprenticeship gained through winning the Prix de Lausanne competition. Yuhui was born in Japan and wanted to come to England to dance professionally: 'I was very interested in the culture of England, and I always wanted to see all the MacMillan pieces and the Ashtons, and to dance in them too.' She remembers her first time on the stage at Covent Garden while still the Prix de Lausanne apprentice, after three years of training in Paris:

> I was just amazed! It was *Swan Lake* Act IV, the first night. The experience was very special. And the House itself is such a wonderful place to be too. When I first came here I had no idea which studio was where. I got lost a few times and it does take a while to get used to it – I still don't know half of what's in the building, and I went into the prop room for the first time only the other day! I love the studios with their high ceilings, and the fact that you can see the sky when you dance.

The prestige of the Royal Opera House and the history and tradition of The Royal Ballet inspire feelings of responsibility in new dancers but also bring opportunities for them to learn with some of the best teachers in the world and among some of the greatest dancers. 'When you're first starting out in a company after being a student, you want to learn as much as you can', explains Eric,

> When I first started dancing as a professional I would try as much as I could to absorb things from other dancers who were already professionals and I watched as much ballet as I could.

And that is one special characteristic of the dance profession: the tremendous value of direct inheritance from the great practitioners of the past. It was Natalia Makarova herself who coached Yuhui for the role of Princess Florine in *The Sleeping Beauty* when she was in her first year with the Company after her apprenticeship: 'What can I say? We get the best people. When we were rehearsing *Jewels* Violette Verdy came to coach us in *Emeralds*!' Verdy, for whom Balanchine pretty much created *Emeralds*, coached Principals including Tamara Rojo and Roberta Marquez. And there have always been guest artists for inspiration too, such as Sylvie Guillem who used to dance with the Company. Yuhui visibly tingles with excitement as she remembers,

> I was in the corps de ballet and I was on the stage with Sylvie when she was dancing Juliet... that was quite special.

54

Like Eric, Yuhui describes the experience of being a professional dancer in the Company as one of direct learning enriched by absorbing the inspirations available: 'I really believe you learn something every day, not just from ballet but from *something*. I'm always inspired by what's going on around me; other people, other things. My eyes are open all the time.' And when one is surrounded by the best one strives to be the best oneself:

> It's the experience of this place, and the things that are around us. For example my role in *Les Sylphides* used to be Margot Fonteyn's role, and that's a really big deal. But Margot is Margot and, well, I'm me! So I always have to find my own way to do it.

Becoming a dancer in The Royal Ballet is also a great deal about developing individually among a large group of very talented young people. At the end of the 2008/9 Season, Yuhui made her debut in *Rubies* and the atmosphere she describes confirms this:

> You feel that the Company is a family. When I gave my debut I could really feel the support from everyone. I love that about this place, and that's how I truly believe I did a good show, because it was not just *me*, but me *plus* everyone else. I truly believe it's not just me – we have to make something together.

The thrill of achievement is a shared as well as an individual experience, and the feeling of familial support among the members of the Company that comes from working so closely with one another towards a shared vision is also experienced by newcomers. Royal Ballet Artist Ruth Bailey is the newest dancer to join the Company; she trained at The Royal Ballet Lower School, White Lodge, and then the

Left: Yuhui in rehearsal for Mikhail Fokine's *Les Sylphides*.
Photograph: Johan Persson

Upper School. She remembers vividly the day she received the news:

> It was December 8th and we were rehearsing *The Nutcracker* for the main stage. I was a student, and many of the students were being rehearsed as snowflakes. I was in my third year of the Upper School, in class, and my teacher Petal Miller took me into Gailene Stock's office, who said they've offered me a job over the road!

Literally over the road, The Royal Ballet Upper School stands next to the Royal Opera House in Floral Street and is connected by a specially designed footbridge – the

55

Right: Monica Mason
rehearses Ruth Bailey
and the corps de ballet
for *Les Sylphides*.
Photograph:
Johan Persson

'Bridge of Aspiration'. The Upper School students use the bridge every day to get to the House for various reasons, from the occasional class with the Company to using the staff and artists' canteen. The students sometimes have the opportunity to take small roles in some of the main stage performances by the Company. Having been a student in the morning, Ruth was suddenly rehearsing that afternoon as a member of The Royal Ballet. 'Everyone was congratulating me – the other students, the corps de ballet, even all the Principals. Everyone', she remembers.

Usually when a dancer is offered a job in the Company it is done at the same time of year as the Company promotions, during or around the tour at the end of the Season, so they have the summer break to sort everything out and then start in September as the new Season's rehearsals begin. However in Ruth's case the process was a little more immediate:

> I had only a few days to get my stuff together, and get my head together. I had the weekend to buy all my new work clothes, and sort my shoes out – sort my life out! It was all very weird because it *is* just across the road but it still felt like I was visiting the Opera House as a student. It took me a good few months to settle in.

Ruth discovered the difference between performing in *Swan Lake* as a student, appearing only in Acts II and IV, and then a few months later appearing as a member of the Company in all four acts, 'quite a different experience'.

As she looks toward her first full Season with the Company – the hard work, the rewards, the expectations – Ruth reflects on the fact that she is one of only four students from her year at the Upper School that have been offered contracts with The Royal Ballet. The rest of her year have all been offered contracts in other ballet companies in the UK and abroad:

> One of my really good friends is joining English National Ballet, so I'm going to live with her next year, and another really good friend is going to Bordeaux, so not too far away... Of course at the School, they always want you to work towards the top, but different dancers suit different companies, and they want you to work to the best of your ability to get the best job you can. When we were at White Lodge I think it was everyone's dream to be in The Royal Ballet, but when you get to the Upper School you realize there are other companies out there. It's a very hard world, the ballet world. But it was always in my mind that this was my ultimate goal.

While fully aware that it is a career, Ruth also knows that in many respects it is a 'dream come true' for a young dancer at the beginning of her profession. Like the more experienced professionals, she is finding her own way too:

> It is hard work, a very hard profession, but it never feels like such an effort because I'm doing what I've always dreamed of doing. At first I didn't think I was supposed to be here – I was just doing a ballet class with The Royal Ballet, and then I was up in the clouds. But it does feel right, like I should be here now; like I'm at home.

Even as a student there was a feeling of responsibility to the Company and as a professional I want to work as hard as I can, look good with the Company and represent them as best I can – oh, and have a ball too! You can't go through life stressing all the time, you've got to have fun, otherwise it will just float past and you'll think: Did I really enjoy it?

Like Yuhui, Ruth feels the powerful inspiration of being among dancers she admires. In some cases they are her teachers. 'When I was at White Lodge I saw quite a few ballets here and I always thought, "I want so much to be on stage with those people".' And then when she joined the Upper School and was given the chance to rehearse with the Company, Ruth remembers, 'there was Tamara, and there was Alina – it was *those people* who I'd seen dance and who I'd fallen in love with, and now I'm sharing the stage with them!'

57

The Agony and the Ecstasy

by Jane Bentham

Nothing symbolizes ballet more obviously than the pointe shoe. All the fairies, magic birds, ghosts, sylphs, sprites and nymphs of classical dance who seem to float, flutter or fly across the stage owe this impression of otherworldly weightlessness to their shoes. Pointe shoes enable the ballerina to dance on the tips of her toes with all her body weight balanced on a small flat surface. Such a device has helped to define the dancer's art as a whole.

At the Royal Opera House around 7000 pairs of pointe shoes are worn each Season, the majority of which are 'stock' shoes that are kept in constant supply in the Pointe Shoe room. Dancers' pointe shoes vary depending on the choreography of the piece being performed: a soft shoe is most appropriate for a lyrical style, while a harder shoe is necessary for a more aggressive style with leaps and turns. For example, during a performance of *Swan Lake* the principal playing Odette/Odile may use up to three pairs of differently adapted pointe shoes (depending upon the choreographic demands of each act), while a dancer from the corps de ballet might need only one pair. It is quite common for a principal dancer to wear out her pointe shoes in a single performance.

Cat Ladd in the Pointe Shoe department at the Royal Opera House explains that 'The work involved in ballet footwear is therefore in two areas: the first is the maintaining of stock footwear, and the second is the fitting and supplying of performance footwear'. Very occasionally the shoes will be kept, but only if they are in some way unique and form part of a costume in the Royal Opera House Collections or if they are of historical interest in terms of design and style. However in most cases they are of little use to anyone after a few performances.

The correct fit is vital. A few millimetres out in the shoe's measurements can make all the difference and dramatically affect the confidence the dancer needs to perform. The pointe shoe must give maximum support to the dancer and an elegant line to her foot.

Since all feet are unique, with variations in strength, arch flexibility, and toe length and shape, shoes are always custom made. Past injuries and place of training also influence the dancer's specifications, as does what she finds aesthetically appealing. The pointe shoe and physiotherapy departments work together with the various manufacturing companies whose individual makers regularly visit the Royal Opera House to make sure they have the right fit. In most cases, a dancer will sample and 'trial' various suppliers, makers and specifications until she has found the ideal shoe. This highly individualized selection process is, of course, very expensive, and the budget for pointe shoes in each Season is approximately £250,000. So it is no surprise that The Royal Ballet Pointe Shoes Appeal has been set up to help with the costs.

Once a dancer has selected her shoes, the brutal 'breaking in' process begins. A new shoe is stiff and inflexible, so various methods must be employed to make it pliable before it can be worn onstage. These range from bending the shoe back and forth to jumping on it, hitting it with a hammer, slamming it in the hinges of a door, and slicing, shaving, scuffing or cutting the sole with a sharp knife. A dancer must be careful not to damage the shoe to such an extent that it becomes too soft and therefore useless. It is a tricky balance to achieve between stiffness and suppleness. As Balanchine put it, 'The pointes for girls have to be, I always say, like an elephant's trunk: strong and yet flexible and soft'.

A dancer may sometimes attempt to 'mould' her shoes to her feet by wearing them after they have been soaked in water. Once the shoes are broken in, she will

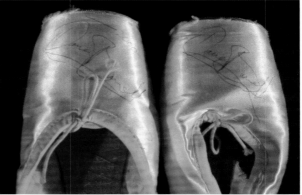

then customize them. This involves sewing on ribbons and sometimes elastics, darning the toe and padding the inside of the toe box with some type of material to protect the toes. The Pointe Shoe department provides lamb's-wool and gel toe pads, but some dancers prefer to use tissue, dishcloths, toe tape and plasters, or nothing at all. This breaking in and customization process takes up a significant amount of time in a dancer's already busy schedule.

It may seem absurd that so much money, time and effort is invested in finding and creating the near perfect pointe shoe. However, it is vital to the ballet dancer's trade, an extension of her legs that makes her art possible. So what exactly constitutes a pointe shoe and how did it come into being?

The two fundamental structural features that allow the dancer to rise onto the tips of her toes are the box – the front of the shoe – and the shank – the sole of the shoe. The box consists of layers of glued paper or burlap that encase the toes and forms a flat end at the front of the shoe so as to provide a platform for the dancer to stand upon. The shank, also made from glued-together paper, supports the arch of the foot when it is en pointe. These 'paper and paste' shoes are slowly being replaced by more modern versions that are made from different types of plastic and are therefore more durable and flexible. Glue, stitching and sometimes small nails bind the shoe together. The outer material is drawn into pleats under the toe and is usually pink satin but can be dyed different colours.

The concept behind pointe shoes began in the late 18th century with the infrequent practice of having dancers suspended from wires. Such a 'flying machine' enabled dancers to rise onto the tips of their toes and then into the air. The suggestion of weightlessness and the ability to

The Agony and the Ecstasy

be airborne was so applauded by audiences that dancers began to search for ways to stand en pointe without relying on wires. In the 1830s dancers started to darn the sides and toe of their satin slippers to give them the greater support needed to use their own foot strength to rise onto their toes. The most famous ballerina of the Romantic period to dance en pointe was Marie Taglioni in *La Sylphide*. Pointe work gave an ethereal quality that was essential to the otherworldly creatures like sylphs and ghosts that were portrayed in the supernatural ballet scenes during this time.

The development of the modern pointe shoe is usually credited to Anna Pavlova at the start of the 20th century. The great Russian ballerina modified her shoes to compensate for the highly arched insteps of her slender feet, which made pointe work for her more of a struggle. She created a shank by inserting a leather sole into her slipper and a box by beating down on the toe area to make it wider and flatter. Pavlova's method of adapting her slippers was considered cheating by her contemporaries; and yet all later 20th-century pointe shoes were based on such a model.

The continuity in pointe shoe design is astonishing, but because their basic construction has changed very little over time they are still tough on the feet. Injuries put aside, common complaints include bruised toenails, bunions, swellings, and metatarsal bruising and strain. Ballerinas suffer a range of ailments that their male counterparts and modern dancers generally avoid. There are two ballets in The Royal Ballet's current repertory that unusually require men to don a pair of pointe shoes: *The Dream* (for Bottom) and *Tales of Beatrix Potter* (for the pigs). Bennet Gartside, a First Soloist who has played the male pointe dancing roles in both of these ballets, says of being en pointe, he has 'never quite felt pain like it before on stage, even with the adrenalin rushing through me at the time'. Dancers must perform through the pain, concealing it under a serene expression. Despite this, the pointe shoe is still the ballerina's timeless tool, with a rich history and long tradition. It may seem a somewhat antiquated, not to mention expensive, part of the dancer's costume – and one that requires much time dedicated to it before it is even 'performance ready'. But ballet would not be what it is without it.

Below: The shelves in the pointe room at the Royal Opera House contain thousands of pairs of pointe shoes.
Photograph: Rob Moore

63

Mayerling

Mayerling

Music
Franz Liszt
Choreography
Kenneth MacMillan

This page: Edward Watson as Crown Prince Rudolph
Photograph: Johan Persson

Previous pages:

Tamara Rojo as Cinderella in *Cinderella*
Photograph: Bill Cooper

Mara Galeazzi and Ryoichi Hirano in *Infra*
Photograph: Bill Cooper

Dancers of The Royal Ballet perform *Symphony in C*
Photograph: Dee Conway

64

The Sleeping Beauty

The Sleeping Beauty

Music
Pyotr Il'yich Tchaikovsky
Choreography
Marius Petipa
Additional Choreography
Frederick Ashton,
Anthony Dowell,
Christopher Wheeldon

Production
Monica Mason
and Christopher Newton
after Ninette de Valois
and Nicholas Sergeyev

Left: Sarah Lamb
as Princess Aurora
and Viacheslav
Samodurov as
Prince Florimund
**Photograph:
Bill Cooper**

65

Agon / Sphinx / New McGregor

**Agon / Sphinx /
New McGregor**

Agon
Music
Igor Stravinsky
Choreography
George Balanchine

Sphinx
Music
Bohuslav Martinů
Choreography
Glen Tetley

New McGregor
Music
Kaija Saariaho
Choreography
Wayne McGregor

Right: Carlos Acosta
in *Agon*
Photograph:
Bill Cooper

Season Preview
2009/10

The Nutcracker

The Nutcracker

Music
Pyotr Il'yich Tchaikovsky
Choreography
Peter Wright
after Lev Ivanov

Production and Scenario
Peter Wright

Left: The Mouse King
Photograph:
Bill Cooper

67

Les Patineurs / Tales of Beatrix Potter

**Les Patineurs /
Tales of Beatrix
Potter**

Les Patineurs
Music
Giacomo Meyerbeer
Choreography
Frederick Ashton

**Tales of Beatrix
Potter**
Music
John Lanchbery
Choreography
Frederick Ashton

Right: Cindy
Jourdain and Laura
McCulloch in *Les
Patineurs*
Photograph:
Johan Persson

Romeo and Juliet

Romeo and Juliet

Music
Sergey Prokofiev
Choreography
Kenneth MacMillan

Left: Alina Cojocaru
as Juliet and Steven
McRae as Romeo
Photograph:
Bill Cooper

69

New Watkins /
Rushes - Fragments of a Lost Story /
Infra

**New Watkins /
Rushes – Fragments
of a Lost Story /
Infra**

New Watkins

Music
Graham Fitkin

Choreography
Jonathan Watkins

**Rushes – Fragments
of a Lost Story**

Music
Sergey Prokofiev
*arranged and elaborated
by* Michael Berkeley

Choreography
Kim Brandstrup

Infra

Music
Max Richter

Choreography
Wayne McGregor

Right: Carlos Acosta
and Laura Morera in
*Rushes - Fragments
of a Lost Story*
**Photograph:
Bill Cooper**

70

La Fille mal gardée

La Fille mal gardée
(The Wayward Daughter)

Music
Ferdinand Hérold
freely adapted
and arranged from
the 1828 version by
John Lanchbery
Choreography
Frederick Ashton

Left: Dancers of
The Royal Ballet
Photograph:
Bill Cooper

71

Concerto / The Judas Tree / Elite Syncopations

**Concerto /
The Judas Tree /
Elite Syncopations**

Concerto
Music
Dmitry Shostakovich
Choreography
Kenneth MacMillan

The Judas Tree
Music
Brian Elias
Choreography
Kenneth MacMillan

Elite Syncopations
Music
Scott Joplin and other
ragtime composers
Choreography
Kenneth MacMillan

Right: Mara Galeazzi,
Thiago Soares and
Ricardo Cervera in
The Judas Tree
Photograph:
Dee Conway

72

Cinderella

Cinderella

Music
Sergey Prokofiev

Choreography
Frederick Ashton

Production
Wendy Ellis Somes

Left: Anthony Dowell and Wayne Sleep as Cinderella's Step-Sisters
Photograph: Dee Conway

73

Electric Counterpoint / New Scarlett / Carmen

Electric Counterpoint / New Scarlett / Carmen

Electric Counterpoint

Music
J.S. Bach, Steve Reich

Choreography
Christopher Wheeldon

New Scarlett

Music
Francis Poulenc

Choreography
Liam Scarlett

Carmen

Music
George Bizet *arranged by* Rodion Shchedrin

Choreography
Mats Ek

Right: Sarah Lamb in *Electric Counterpoint*
Photograph:
Dee Conway

74

Chroma / Tryst / Symphony in C

Chroma / Tryst / Symphony in C

Chroma
Music
Joby Talbot,
Jack White III *arranged by* Joby Talbot
and orchestrated by Christopher Austin
Choreography
Wayne McGregor

Tryst
Music
James MacMillan
Choreography
Christopher Wheeldon

Symphony in C
Music
Georges Bizet
Choreography
George Balanchine

Left: Dancers of The Royal Ballet in *Tryst*
Photograph:
Bill Cooper

75

MacMillan Magic

by Jann Parry

Had Kenneth MacMillan lived, he would have been 80 at the end of 2009. His life was cut short by a heart attack at the age of 62, during the first night of a revival of his ballet *Mayerling* in 1992. The Royal Ballet performs a run of *Mayerling* in the autumn of 2009, with a performance on 29 October, the exact anniversary of his death. This latest revival is part of a Season that further honours MacMillan with the return of his *Romeo and Juliet* at the start of the new year and a mixed programme of his ballets in March and April 2010.

The five very different works give a sense of how wide-ranging his subjects and styles of choreography could be. He created well over sixty ballets and gala *pas de deux*, and had yet more works planned when he died so tragically backstage. In his last years, he had created *Winter Dreams*, *The Prince of the Pagodas*, *The Judas Tree* and dances for the National Theatre's production of *Carousel* – works spanning classical ballet, biblical allegory and Broadway musical theatre. Like all his creations, they sprang from sources that had formed his career as a maker of dances.

Ideas had poured out of him as soon as he started to choreograph in the 1950s, following a period of severe stage fright as a performer. Ninette de Valois had given him leave of absence from her Covent Garden ballet company in order to recover, proposing he should then rejoin the second, touring company. In the interim, he was invited by his friend John Cranko to join an ad hoc group of dancers in Henley-on-Thames over the summer of 1953. Cranko had been asked by the artist John Piper to help bring the disused Kenton Theatre back to life with an entertaining programme of dance. During the hot, happy summer, Cranko encouraged MacMillan to think of himself as a possible choreographer. After returning to the touring company as a dancer, MacMillan tried his hand at a ballet

76

for the first experimental Sadler's Wells Choreographers' Group. The result, *Somnambulism*, was the talking-point of the evening. Set to jazz records by Stan Kenton, it was reprised in 1956, this time with live music, as part of an all-MacMillan evening – the first time the ten-year-old 'junior' company had programmed a mixed programme by a single choreographer, who was also one of its own.

The other ballets were *Danses concertantes*, MacMillan's first professional commission from 1955, and a new ballet, *Solitaire*, which was soon taken into the repertory of both companies. Still in his mid-twenties, MacMillan had staked his claim as a choreographer to watch, already a rival to the more experienced Cranko and, eventually, to Frederick Ashton. De Valois kept a watchful eye on her promising protégé, advising him on his scenarios for ballets and on the kind of music she thought he should use: no more jazz, and avoid a harpsichord – too difficult to tour. He had the confidence to ignore her suggestions and even to override her objection to the rape scene in his 1960 ballet, *The Invitation*, with a young Lynn Seymour as the traumatized heroine.

Many of his ideas came from films, often sending him back to the books that had inspired the film-makers. Kenneth had been an inveterate film-goer since childhood, a passion that distinguished him from an older generation of choreographers less obsessed with the screen. He thought in vivid images, filling the stage with action and isolating his characters in stillness as if for a close-up. Wanting swift scene changes like cinematic jump cuts, he was thwarted by the cumbersome procedures backstage in the Royal Opera House (it was a few years after his death that the theatre was redeveloped and its stage facilities modernized). He was further frustrated by audience expectations that ballet stories should unfold

Previous page: Anne Heaton, Donald Britton and Margaret Hill in *Somnambulism* (1956)
Photograph: Denis de Marney/ Theatre Collection/ V&A Images

This page: Maryon Lane and David Poole in *Danses concertantes* (1955)
Photograph: Denis de Marney/ Theatre Collection/ V&A Images

77

should never flinch from addressing the demanding concerns that playwrights take on, MacMillan believed: dance need not be removed from reality, for it can examine disturbed personalities, intolerable pressures, betrayal and guilt. He drew on his own experience of psychoanalysis to explore on stage what the dance critic Clement Crisp has called 'the interior landscapes and labyrinths of the psyche'.

A child of war, and of the Cold War that followed the end of World War II's hostilities, MacMillan was always looking for ways to deal with his awareness of its consequences. *The Burrow* (1958) was about persecuted people living in dread of discovery; *Gloria* (1980) lamented the waste of young lives in battle; *Valley of Shadows* (1983) confronted the horror of concentration camps, offending many audience members' sensibilities; *Different Drummer* (1984), based on Büchner's *Woyzeck*, anatomized the institutionalized cruelty of an army.

conventionally, instead of starting in the middle or even the end, as films often do. In *Mayerling*, for example, he and his scenarist, Gillian Freeman (who has worked as a writer of film scripts), opened the ballet with the funeral of a character whose identity becomes clear only in the final scene. His last, tantalizing work, *The Judas Tree*, takes place in multiple time zones, past, present and future overlapping.

As well as films, MacMillan was influenced by the theatre, from the angry young Royal Court rebels of the 1950s, such as John Osborne and Arnold Wesker, to the surrealist experiments of Ionesco and Büchner. Ballet

78

When MacMillan moved to West Berlin, where he was artistic director of the Deutsche Oper Ballet from 1966 to 1969, he was constantly reminded of the presence of the military in the divided city. In *Concerto* (1966), one of his first works for the German company, the corps de ballet swirl like soldiers on parade, the women swinging their arms light-heartedly as they strut on point. In his one-act *Anastasia*, created a year later, the heroine's terror of armed men is relived in an asylum as she tries to assert her identity. The woman who claimed to be Anastasia had been interned in an asylum in Berlin, and was still bringing legal cases before the German courts while MacMillan was living in the city.

The surveillance of border guards, to which he had been subjected when travelling in and out of West Berlin, appeared in his ballet *Checkpoint*, when he returned to take over The Royal Ballet in 1970. Based on George Orwell's *1984*, its subject was a pair of doomed lovers fleeing the all-seeing eye of Big Brother. They were a futuristic incarnation of Romeo and Juliet, crushed by the pitiless demands of an oppressive society.

However Expressionist his approach in a number of works, MacMillan continued to rely on the technique of classical ballet as his physical language. He was convinced that its extensive vocabulary could be adapted to convey extremes of emotion.

Left: Mara Galeazzi as Anna Anderson in *Anastasia* (2004)
Photograph: Bill Cooper

79

MacMillan Magic

He required dancers to abandon decorum in favour of passion, pushing themselves to the limit. His roles offer challenges that performers around the world are eager to take up. But he was also adept at choreographing non-narrative ballets, relying for inspiration on his choice of music: *Concerto*, to Shostakovich, and *Danses Concertantes*, to Stravinsky, are just two of them. *Elite Syncopations* was his response to ragtime rhythms by Scott Joplin and other American composers, created for light relief in 1974 after the completion of *Manon*. Although *Elite Syncopation*'s comedy might seem unusual, compared with the high drama of much of the rest of MacMillan's work, he choreographed other irreverent pieces: a burlesque duet, *Side Show*, originally for Rudolf Nureyev and Lynn Semour; *Valse Eccentrique* (1960), a comic trio for Anya Linden and two male Edwardian bathers; the duet for the drunken Lescaut and his forbearing mistress in *Manon*.

During his career, MacMillan created three different versions of *The Seven Deadly Sins*, Weill's and Brecht's satirical 'sung ballet'. The show provided opportunities to exploit a variety of dance styles, from tap to burlesque and popular crazes. As a boy in Great Yarmouth, MacMillan had tap-danced on the end of the pier, dreaming of becoming a star like Fred Astaire. He loved musicals, and was delighted to be involved in the National Theatre's 1992 production of *Carousel*, just before he died. Its director, Nicholas Hytner, had invited him to be the choreographer for all its routines as well as the dream ballet near the end. '*Carousel* is about sex and violence', Hytner explained. 'That's what I do', replied MacMillan laconically... and laughed.

Jann Parry is the author of the new biography *Different Drummer: the Life of Kenneth MacMillan*, published by Faber & Faber

81

1930s

1931 20 January Bizet's opera *Carmen* is staged at the newly reopened Sadler's Wells Theatre. The dancers in it come from a fledgling ballet company, the Vic-Wells Opera Ballet, under the creative direction of their founder Ninette De Valois. The result of many developments of this Company – always under De Valois' leadership – would eventually be The Royal Ballet. **5 May** The Company gives its own performance of short works by De Valois at Lilian Baylis's Old Vic theatre. It is Baylis's use of dancers in her operas and plays that gives De Valois the chance to bring her Company together. **July** The Camargo Society presents the Company in a programme which includes De Valois' *Job* and two works by Frederick Ashton, a young dancer also beginning to make his mark as a choreographer.

1932 January Alicia Markova becomes a regular Guest Artist alongside Anton Dolin. **March** *Les Sylphides* is revived with Markova and Dolin. **September** The Company tours for the first time together, to Denmark. **October** Act II of *Le Lac des cygnes* marks the Company's first foray into the classical repertory.

1933 March Nicholas Sergeyev presents the full-length *Coppélia* with Lydia Lopokova as Swanilda. He had been the *régisseur general* of the Mariinsky Theatre, but fled Russia after the October Revolution bringing the written notation necessary to stage many classic Russian ballets.

1934 January Sergeyev puts on *Giselle* with Markova and Dolin. **April** *Casse-Noisette* is presented, again by Sergeyev. **20 November** The full *Le Lac des cygnes* is presented with Markova and Robert Helpmann, who had recently been promoted to Principal with the Company.

1935 Ashton is signed up as a performer and resident choreographer. **20 May** De Valois' *The Rake's Progress* has its first performance, with Markova as the Betrayed Girl. **26 November** Ashton's *Le Baiser de la fée* receives its premiere, with the young Margot Fonteyn in the cast.

1937 The Company represents British culture at the International Exhibition in Paris. **16 February** The premiere of Ashton's *Les Patineurs*. **27 April** A further Ashton premiere with *A Wedding Bouquet*.

5 October De Valois' *Checkmate* receives its first performance in London. **25 November** Lilian Baylis dies.

1939 2 February Sergeyev puts on *The Sleeping Princess* with Fonteyn and Helpmann in the lead roles. **1 September** Germany invades Poland; in response, Britain, France, Australia and New Zealand declare war on Germany.

1940s

1940 23 January The first performance of Ashton's *Dante Sonata*. **May** The Company travels to the Netherlands for a small tour, but the advancing German army forces a hurried escape. **November** The Company begins to tour throughout wartime Britain.

1941 The New Theatre, St Martin's Lane, becomes the Company's home for much of the war, and *The Sleeping Princess* is again staged.

1942 19 May The first performance of Helpmann's ballet *Hamlet*, with Helpmann in the title role.

1944 26 October Helpmann's *Miracle in the Gorbals* receives its premiere.

1945 The Company undertakes a tour of the Continent with the Entertainments National Service Association (ENSA), a forces organization. **May 8th** The war ends in Europe.

1946 20 February The Company becomes resident at Covent Garden, and re-opens the Royal Opera House with *The Sleeping Beauty*. **24 April** Ashton's *Symphonic Variations* is performed for the first time.

1947 February De Valois invites Léonide Massine, one of the biggest stars of Diaghilev's Ballets Russes, to revive *The Three-Cornered Hat* and *La Boutique fantasque*.

1948 23 December Ashton's *Cinderella* receives its premiere: it is the Company's first home-grown full-length ballet.

1949 9 October The Company presents *The Sleeping Beauty* in New York, the start of a hugely successful tour that takes in many cities in the USA and Canada.

Top: Pamela May and Harold Turner in *Checkmate* (1937)
Photograph: Frank Sharman Collection/ Royal Opera House Collections

Bottom: Margot Fonteyn and Michael Somes in Frederick Ashton's *Dante Sonata* (1947)
Photograph: Frank Sharman Collection/ Royal Opera House Collections

Below: Moira Shearer in *Cinderella* (1948)
Photograph: Roger Wood Collection/ Royal Opera House Collections

Royal Ballet Yearbook 2009/10

1950s

1950 20 February The first performance of De Valois' *Don Quixote.* **5 April** George Balanchine and his New York City Ballet make their first European visit, Balanchine reviving his *Ballet Imperial* for Sadler's Wells Ballet. **5 May** Roland Petit's creation for the Company, *Ballabile,* receives its premiere. **September** The Company embarks on a five-month, 32-city tour of the USA.

1951 21 August Music Director Constant Lambert, one of the chief architects of the Company with De Valois and Ashton, dies aged 45.

1952 3 September The first performance of Ashton's *Sylvia.*

1953 2 June Coronation gala for HM The Queen, which includes a specially devised ballet by Ashton for the occasion, *Homage to the Queen.*

1954 23 August For the 25th anniversary of Diaghilev's death, the Company joins the Edinburgh Festival tributes with a performance of *The Firebird*; Fonteyn dances the title role.

1956 1 March Kenneth MacMillan creates his first ballet for the Sadler's Wells Ballet, *Noctambules.* **31 October** The Sadler's Wells Ballet, the Sadler's Wells Theatre Ballet and the School are granted a Royal Charter – the main Company becoming The Royal Ballet.

1957 1 January John Cranko's *The Prince of the Pagodas*, to a score by Benjamin Britten, is given its first performance at Covent Garden. It is the first full-length work to a modern commissioned score to be presented in the West.

1958 27 October Ashton's new ballet *Ondine*, created for Fonteyn, opens with her in the title role; the new score is by Hans Werner Henze.

1959 13 March MacMillan's *Danses concertantes*, created for Sadler's Wells Theatre Ballet in 1955, opens at Covent Garden.

1960s

1960 28 January The premiere of Ashton's 'tribute to nature', *La Fille mal gardée* with Nadia Nerina dancing the role of Lise to David Blair's Colas. (See Great Dancers of The Royal Ballet, page 90.)

1961 15 June The Company makes its first tour of Russia presenting *Ondine* on the first night; an exchange agreement sees the Kirov Ballet perform at Covent Garden.

1962 21 February Rudolf Nureyev, having controversially defected from the Bolshoi in 1961, makes his debut as Albrecht to Fonteyn's Giselle. **3 May** MacMillan's new version of *The Rite of Spring*, with Monica Mason as the Chosen Maiden, is given its first performance.

1963 12 March Ashton's *Marguerite and Armand*, created for Fonteyn and Nureyev, opens. **7 May** De Valois retires as Director of the Company and Ashton succeeds her, while De Valois becomes supervisor of The Royal Ballet School. **28 November** Nureyev's first staging for The Royal Ballet is the 'Kingdom of the Shades' scene from *La Bayadère*.

1964 29 February Antoinette Sibley dances Aurora in the Company's 400th performance of *The Sleeping Beauty*. **2 April** The Company's contributions to the celebrations of the 400th anniversary of Shakespeare's birth include Ashton's *The Dream*, which launches the dance partnership of Sibley and Anthony Dowell. **2 December** Bronislava Nijinska, younger sister of Nijinsky, revives her *Les Biches*, with Svetlana Beriosova as the Hostess.

1965 9 February MacMillan's first full-length work, *Romeo and Juliet*, is presented; created for Lynn Seymour and Christopher Gable, the opening night is danced by Fonteyn and Nureyev.

1966 23 March Nijinska revives her *Les Noces* in a double bill with *Les Biches*. **May** MacMillan takes up the ballet directorship of the Deutsche Oper Berlin. **19 May** MacMillan's *Song of the Earth*, created for Cranko's Stuttgart Ballet, is given its Covent Garden premiere.

1967 25 January Antony Tudor creates his first work for The Royal Ballet, *Shadowplay*.

Top: Margot Fonteyn and Rudolf Nureyev in *Giselle* (1962)
Photograph: Zoë Dominic

Bottom: Antoinette Sibley and Anthony Dowell in *The Dream* (1964)
Photograph: Houston Rogers/ Theatre Collection/ V&A Images

Below: Svetlana Beriosova in *Les Biches* (1964)
Photograph: Houston Rogers/ Theatre Collection/ V&A Images

85

1968 29 February The premiere of Nureyev's version of
The Nutcracker. **26 April** The Company makes the official
announcement of Ashton's retirement as Director in 1970 and his
succession by MacMillan. **25 October** The premiere of Ashton's
Enigma Variations. **12 November** Tudor revives his 1938
production of *Lilac Garden*.

1970s

1971 22 July MacMillan's long-awaited *Anastasia* opens, with
Seymour in the lead role. **4 August** The premiere of American
choreographer Glen Tetley's contemporary ballet *Field Figures*.

1972 20 June Natalia Makarova dances Giselle, partnered by
Dowell, making her debut at Covent Garden as a Guest Artist.

1973 8 June At Covent Garden, Nureyev and Makarova dance
The Sleeping Beauty together for the first time.

1974 7 March Sibley, Dowell and David Wall dance the opening
night of MacMillan's *Manon*. **7 October** The premiere of
MacMillan's *Elite Syncopations* with Wayne Sleep in the Principal
Character role. (See Great Dancers of The Royal Ballet, page 90.)

1975 April The Royal Ballet makes its first tour of the Far East.

1976 12 February The first performance of Ashton's *A Month in
the Country*, with Dowell and Seymour.

1977 13 June Norman Morrice succeeds MacMillan as Director of
The Royal Ballet.

1978 14 February The premiere of MacMillan's full-length ballet
Mayerling, the Principal male role created for Irek Mukhamedov.
(See Great Dancers of The Royal Ballet, page 91.)

1980s

1980 13 March MacMillan's *Gloria* receives its premiere.
4 August Ashton creates *Rhapsody* for Lesley Collier and Mikhail
Baryshnikov, given at a performance for the 80th birthday of HM
Queen Elizabeth The Queen Mother.

1981 30 April World premiere of MacMillan's *Isadora* with Merle
Park in the title role, to celebrate the Company's golden jubilee.

86

1982 2 December The premiere of Nureyev's *The Tempest*.

1984 24 February MacMillan's *Different Drummer* is created for the Company. **20 December** Collier and Dowell perform in the first night of Peter Wright's Biedermeier-inspired production of *The Nutcracker*.

1986 Anthony Dowell is appointed Director of The Royal Ballet.

1987 12 March *Swan Lake*, with Cynthia Harvey and Jonathan Cope, is Dowell's first production as Director. **16 December** Ashton stages a revival of *Cinderella*, his final production for The Royal Ballet.

1988 9 March Bintley's *'Still Life' at the Penguin Café* receives its world premiere with the Company. **19 August** Ashton dies in the year in which his *Ondine* is revived by Dowell after an absence of 22 years from the repertory.

1989 18 May The full-length *La Bayadère* is first given by The Royal Ballet in a new production by Makarova. **8 December** MacMillan's final, full-evening production, *The Prince of the Pagodas*, is created for the Company, with Darcey Bussell and Jonathan Cope.

1990s

1990 19 July MacMillan's *'Farewell' pas de deux* with Bussell and Irek Mukhamedov is performed at a London Palladium gala.

1991 7 February The first night of MacMillan's *Winter Dreams* (which grew out of the *'Farewell' pas de deux*) . **2 May** In celebration of the 60th anniversary of the Company, Bintley's *Cyrano* is first performed at a Royal Gala.

1992 13 February William Forsythe's *In the middle, somewhat elevated* is first performed by the Company. **19 March** MacMillan's last work, *The Judas Tree*, created for Mukhamedov and Viviana Durante, receives its premiere. **29 October** MacMillan dies of a heart attack at the first performance of a major revival of his *Mayerling*. **6 December** Ashton's *Tales of Beatrix Potter* is first staged live by The Royal Ballet.

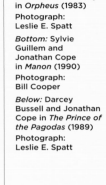

Top: Peter Schaufuss and Jennifer Penney in *Orpheus* (1983)
Photograph: Leslie E. Spatt

Bottom: Sylvie Guillem and Jonathan Cope in *Manon* (1990)
Photograph: Bill Cooper

Below: Darcey Bussell and Jonathan Cope in *The Prince of the Pagodas* (1989)
Photograph: Leslie E. Spatt

87

1993 7 April Baryshnikov's *Don Quixote* is first performed by the Company in new designs.

1994 6 April A new production of *The Sleeping Beauty* by Anthony Dowell is performed in Washington in the presence of the President of the USA and HRH The Princess Margaret.
18 June Ashley Page's *Fearful Symmetries* is first performed (receiving the 1995 Olivier Award for Best New Dance Production).
3 November Dowell's production of *The Sleeping Beauty* with designs by Maria Björnson is first performed at the Royal Opera House for a Royal Gala.

1996 2 May MacMillan's *Anastasia* is performed with new sets and costumes by Bob Crowley.

1997 14 July Farewell Gala and final performance at the 'old' Royal Opera House. During the closure The Royal Ballet is 'on tour', performing at Labatt's Apollo, Hammersmith, the Royal Festival Hall and the Barbican.

1999 December The redeveloped Royal Opera House opens. The Royal Ballet's first programme is 'A Celebration of International Choreography' **17 December** The opening night of *The Nutcracker* is the first performance of a full-length ballet in the new House.

2000s
2000 8 February Revival of De Valois' production of *Coppélia* in the original designs by Osbert Lancaster opens. **29 February** Ashton's *Marguerite and Armand* is revived with Sylvie Guillem and Nicolas Le Riche in the title roles. **6 May** Millicent Hodson and Kenneth Archer produce a major restaging of Nijinsky's *Jeux* in a programme with *L'Après-midi d'un faune*.

2001 8 March De Valois dies. **July** Dowell retires as Director of The Royal Ballet. **23 October** The first performance of Nureyev's version of *Don Quixote* by The Royal Ballet, which marks the first performance under Ross Stretton's tenure as Director.
22 November The first performance by The Royal Ballet of Cranko's *Onegin*.

2002 9 February HRH The Princess Margaret, Countess of Snowdon, President of The Royal Ballet, dies. **September** Ross Stretton resigns as Director. **December** Monica Mason becomes Director of the Company.

2003 13 January The Company dances Jiří Kylián's *Sinfonietta* for the first time. **8 March** The premiere of Makarova's new production of *The Sleeping Beauty*. **22 December** Wendy Ellis Somes's new production of *Cinderella* receives its premiere.

2004 April The Royal Ballet pays homage to Serge Diaghilev in a 75th anniversary tribute programme that includes the Company premiere of *Le Spectre de la rose*. **4 November** The premiere of Ashton's full-length *Sylvia*, reconstructed and staged by Christopher Newton for the 'Ashton 100' celebrations.

2005 7 May The premiere of a new work by Christopher Bruce, inspired by the life of Jimi Hendrix: *Three Songs – Two Voices*.

2006 15 May The Company begins its 75th anniversary celebrations with a new production of the 1946 *Sleeping Beauty*, realized by Monica Mason and Christopher Newton with Messel's original designs, re-created by Peter Farmer, followed by revivals of Ashton's *Homage to The Queen*, with additional new choreography by Christopher Wheeldon, Michael Corder and David Bintley, and De Valois' *The Rake's Progress*. **8 June** A gala performance of *Homage* preceded by *La Valse* and *divertissements* is attended by HM The Queen. **November** The premieres of Wayne McGregor's *Chroma* and Wheeldon's *DGV: Danse à grande vitesse*. **December** McGregor becomes Resident Choreographer of The Royal Ballet.

2007 March Alastair Marriott's *Children of Adam* receives its premiere. **April** Will Tuckett's *The Seven Deadly Sins* receives its premiere. **June** Barry Wordsworth is appointed Music Director. **8 June** Darcey Bussell retires as a Principal. **23 November** The Royal Ballet performs Balanchine's *Jewels* in its entirety for the first time.

2008 28 February The first performance of Wheeldon's *Electric Counterpoint*. **23 April** The mainstage choreographic debut of Kim Brandstrup with *Rushes – Fragments of a Lost Story*. **15 June to 21 July** The Royal Ballet goes on tour in China and the Far East, performing in Beijing, Shanghai, Tokyo, Osaka and

Left: Alina Cojocaru and Johann Kobborg in *Onegin* (2004) Photograph: Dee Conway

Hong Kong. **October** marks the 50th anniversary of Ashton's *Ondine*. **13 November** The premiere of McGregor's *Infra*.

2009 March Anthony Russell Roberts retires as Artistic Administrator and is succeeded by Kevin O'Hare. **April** Jeanetta Laurence is appointed Associate Director of The Royal Ballet. **June–July** The Royal Ballet tours to Washington D.C., Granada and Havana.

89

NADIA NERINA

Nadia Nerina's dancing was especially noted for its virtuosity, buoyant jumps, lightness of foot and sunny demeanour, all of which made her the perfect ballerina to create the role of Lise in Frederick Ashton's bucolic masterpiece, *La Fille mal gardée*. The first performances were in 1960, when Nerina danced the title role opposite her long-standing dance partner David Blair as Colas. This was far from her only ballet for Ashton, and as one of his favourite performers he also created roles for her in *Cinderella*, *Homage to The Queen*, *Variations on a Theme by Purcell* and *Birthday Offering*. She also created new roles in Kenneth MacMillan's *Noctambules*, Robert Helpmann's *Elektra*, Peter Darrell's *Home* and Andrée Howard's *Mardi gras*. Other of her leading roles included those in *Sylvia*, *The Sleeping Beauty*, *Ondine*, *Coppélia*, *Giselle* and *Swan Lake*.

Although her professional career was strongly based in London and with its ballet companies, she had in fact been born in Cape Town in 1927 and began her ballet training in South Africa. She moved to London in 1945 and studied at both the Rambert School and Sadler's Wells Ballet School. The following year she joined Sadler's Wells Theatre Ballet, then in 1947 joined Sadler's Wells Ballet (which later became The Royal Ballet) as a Soloist, and by 1952 had been promoted to Principal. Nerina left her permanent position with The Royal Ballet at the end of the 1965 Season to become a freelance Guest Artist and went on to appear with the Bolshoi and the Kirov, although she continued to make guest appearances with The Royal Ballet until her retirement at the end of the decade. A few years later she moved to France, where she died in October 2008.

Above: Nadia Nerina as Lise in *La Fille mal gardée* (1960)
Photograph: Houston Rogers/ Theatre Collection/ V&A Images

Right: Wayne Sleep as Puck in *The Dream* (1968)
Photograph: Anthony Crickmay/ Theatre Collection/ V&A Images

90

WAYNE SLEEP

A distinctive combination of talents made Wayne Sleep one of the most widely recognized and popular dancers of his generation, in the process spreading the enjoyment and appreciation of dance beyond the conventional ballet theatre. His energy and speed along with his short stature and natural stage presence made him perfect for roles that combined virtuoso technique and a distinctive characterization (often through humour as in *Elite Syncopations*, where he was paired with a much taller female dancer to play on their difference in height). He was also very popular as Puck in *The Dream* and, later in his career, as one of the Step-Sisters in *Cinderella*, both by Ashton.

Sleep was born in Plymouth, in 1948, trained at the Royal Ballet Schools and joined the Company in 1966, becoming a Principal in 1973. He performed many major roles, including ones created by Frederick Ashton for him in *Jazz Calendar* and *Enigma Variations* (1968) and *A Month in the Country* (1976), and by Kenneth MacMillan in *Anastasia* (1971), *Elite Syncopations* and *Manon* (1964) and *The Four Seasons* (1975). Beyond The Royal Ballet, he formed the dance company DASH, which performed in the West End and internationally and he appeared in the West End in the original productions of Lloyd Webber's *Cats* and *Song and Dance* and as the Emcee in a revival of *Cabaret*.

Sleep has also been an actor on stage as well as in radio, television and film, and has choreographed his own works, which include *David and Goliath* (London Contemporary Dance, San Francisco Ballet), *Savoy Suite* (English National Ballet), *Soldier's Tale* and *The Hot Shoe Show* (BBC television and stage), *Carousel* and works for National Youth Ballet. In 1998 he was awarded an OBE and established his own charity, The Wayne Sleep Dance Scholarship.

IREK MUKHAMEDOV

Irek Mukhamedov first made his name in his native Russia, but international touring brought him a world-wide reputation as one of the most admired dancers of his time. Mukhamedov was not a typical danseur noble (someone who takes on such roles as the Prince in classical ballets) but his performances were always strongly focused, with his physical power and heroic style making him ideal for a variety of repertory which included Albrecht, Romeo, Cyrano, Solor, Petrushka, Jean de Brienne, Faun, Prodigal Son and in *Les Biches*.

Born in Kazan in 1960, Mukhamedov trained at the Moscow Choreographic Institute and then joined the Classical Ballet Company, with whom he quickly made his name. He made his debut with the Bolshoi in Grigorovich's *Spartacus* (1981) and soon became a favourite dancer of the director. In 1990 he left Russia and joined The Royal Ballet as a Principal, becoming a Guest Artist in 1998. In a new country and with a new ballet company,

Mukhamedov found a sympathetic mentor in Kenneth MacMillan, who created roles for him in *Winter Dreams* (1991) and *The Judas Tree* (1992), and also gave him the opportunity to dance the leading roles in *Manon* (1991) and *Mayerling* (1992). Other leading roles Mukhamedov created were in Twyla Tharp's *Mister Worldly-Wise*, William Tuckett's *The Crucible* and *The Turn of the Screw* and Ashley Page's *Fearful Symmetries* and *now langorous, now wild*. Although more recently he has danced Zorba (*Zorba the Greek*) in Verona, he has also concentrated on choreography – *Swan Lake*, *Sabres 'n' Roses*, *Four Horsemen* and *The Prince and the Pauper* are some of his own works. He has won many prizes, including the Andersen Prize for Best Dancer (1988), and in 2000 he was awarded an OBE. Since 2007 he has been Artistic Director of the Greek National Opera Ballet.

Left:
Irek Mukhamedov as Basilio in *Don Quixote* (1993)
Photograph: Leslie E. Spatt

91

Recordings

SELECTED RECORDINGS OF THE ROYAL BALLET ON DVD AND BLU-RAY

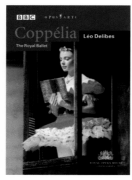

Coppélia
Music: Delibes
Choreography: De Valois
Cast: Benjamin, Acosta, Heydon
The Orchestra of the Royal Opera House/
Moldoveanu
Recorded 2000
DVD: Opus Arte OA0831D
All regions (NTSC)

La Fille mal gardée
Music: Hérold (arr. Lanchbery)
Choreography: Ashton
Cast: Nuñez, Acosta, Tuckett, Howells
The Orchestra of the Royal Opera House/Twiner
Recorded 2005
DVD: Opus Arte OA0992D
All regions (NTSC)
Blu-ray: BBC Opus Arte OABD7021D
All regions (NTSC)

The Firebird and Les Noces
Music: Stravinsky
Choreography: Fokine / Nijinska
Cast: Benjamin, Cope / Yanowsky, Pickering
The Orchestra of the Royal Opera House/Carewe
Recorded 2001
Plus: film of Stravinsky conducting
The Firebird Suite
DVD: Opus Arte OA0832D
All regions (NTSC)

Giselle
Music: Adam
Choreography: Petipa
Cast: Cojocaru, Kobborg, Nuñez, Harvey
The Orchestra of the Royal Opera House/Gruzin
Recorded 2006
DVD: Opus Arte OA0993D
All regions (NTSC)
Blu-ray: Opus Arte OABD7030D

The Judas Tree
Music: Elias
Choreography: MacMillan
Cast: Mukhamedov, Benjamin, Nunn
The Orchestra of the Royal Opera House/
Wordsworth
Recorded 1997
Plus: Birmingham Royal Ballet in Bintley's
Nutcracker Sweeties
DVD: NVC Arts 3984-24313
Region coding: 2,3,4,5 (NTSC)

Mayerling
Music: Liszt
Choreography: MacMillan
Cast: Mukhamedov, Durante, Collier, Bussell
The Orchestra of the Royal Opera House/
Wordsworth
Recorded 1994
DVD: Opus Arte OAR3101D
All regions (NTSC)

Manon
Music: Massenet
Choreography: MacMillan
Cast: Rojo, Acosta, Martin, Saunders
The Orchestra of the Royal Opera House/
Martin Yates
Recorded 2008
DVD: Decca
All regions (NTSC)

The Nutcracker
Music: Tchaikovsky
Choreography: Ivanov, Wright
Cast: Dowell, Cojocaru, Putrov, Yoshida, Cope
The Orchestra of the Royal Opera House/
Svetlanov
Recorded 2000
DVD: Opus Arte OA0827D
All regions (NTSC)

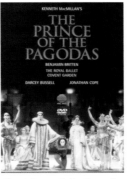

The Prince of the Pagodas
Music: Britten
Choreography: MacMillan
Cast: Bussell, Cope, Chadwick, Dowell, Rice,
Dowson, Sansom, Silver, Page
The Orchestra of the Royal Opera House/
Lawrence
Recorded 1989
DVD: NVC Arts 9031-73826-2
Region coding: 2,3,4,5 (NTSC)

Romeo and Juliet
Music Prokofiev
Choreography: MacMillan
Cast: Rojo, Acosta, Martin, Soares
Royal Ballet Sinfonia/Boris Gruzin
Recorded: 2007
DVD: Decca
All regions (NTSC)

The Sleeping Beauty
Music: Tchaikovsky
Choreography: Petipa, Ashton, Dowell,
Wheeldon
Cast: Cojocaru, Bonelli, Saunders, McGorian,
Marriott, Rosato, Nuñez
The Orchestra of the Royal Opera House/
Ovsyanikov
Recorded 2007
DVD: Opus Arte OA0995D
All regions (NTSC)

This is just a selection of the wide range of Royal Ballet productions captured on DVD and Blu-Ray. Productions are recorded for future release each Season, while archive recordings continue to be re-released.

www.roh.org.uk/rbshop

Books

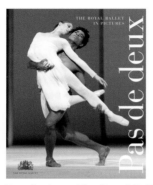

Pas de deux: The Royal Ballet in Pictures

Over 200 photographs of 53 ballets, in rehearsal and performance.

Oberon Books, 2007

ISBN 978-1-84002-777-8

In House

In House, photographs of The Royal Ballet by Bill Cooper, records the first three years of performances in the newly refurbished Royal Opera House. Over 200 photographs of 43 ballets are featured.

Oberon Books, 2002

ISBN 1-84002-350-3

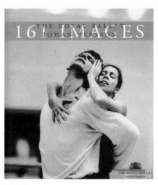

161 Images

Black and white photographs of The Royal Ballet by former dancer Johan Persson, taken during the 2002/3 season, in rehearsal, on stage and in the wings.

Oberon Books, 2003

ISBN 1-84002-374-0

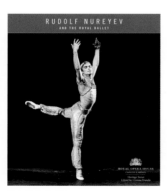

Rudolph Nureyev and The Royal Ballet

Black and white photographs documenting Rudolph Nureyev's long association with The Royal Ballet, edited by Cristina Franchi.

Oberon Books, 2005

ISBN 1-84002-462-3

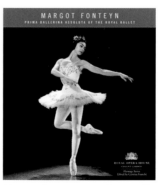

Margot Fonteyn: Prima Ballerina Assoluta of The Royal Ballet

Black and white photographs documenting Dame Margot Fonteyn's long association with The Royal Ballet, edited by Cristina Franchi.

Oberon Books, 2004

ISBN 1-84002-460-7

Frederick Ashton: Founder Choreographer of The Royal Ballet

Black and white photographs documenting Sir Frederick Ashton's career and ballets made for The Royal Ballet, edited by Cristina Franchi.

Oberon Books, 2004

ISBN 1-84002-461-5

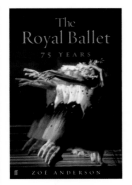

The Royal Ballet: 75 years

By Zoë Anderson

A history of The Royal Ballet since its inception to the present day.

Faber & Faber, 2006

ISBN 0-571-22795-3

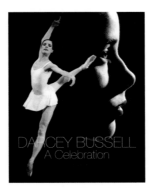

Darcey Bussell: A Celebration

By Clive Burton

A pictorial celebration of the career and life of Darcey Bussell.

Reynolds & Hearne, 2008

ISBN 978-1-905287-92-5

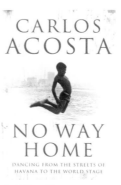

No Way Home

By Carlos Acosta

Acosta tells his life story from the streets of Cuba to the ballet stages of the world.

HarperCollins, 2008

ISBN 978-0-00-7255078-3

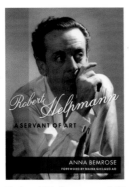

Robert Helpmann: A Servant of Art

By Anna Bemrose

A comprehensive biography of Sir Robert Helpmann, detailing his life in dance, film and theatre.

UQP, 2009

ISBN 978-0-7022-3678-5

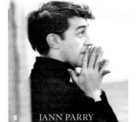

Different Drummer: The Life of Kenneth MacMillan

By Jann Parry

The first complete biography of Kenneth MacMillan.

Faber & Faber, 2009

ISBN 0-571-24302-9

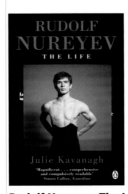

Rudolf Nureyev: The Life

By Julie Kavanagh

The authorized biography of Rudolf Nureyev.

Penguin, 2008

ISBN 978-0-14-102969-6

Freddy

OFFICIAL SPONSOR AND SUPPLIER OF DANCE FITNESS WEAR TO THE ROYAL BALLET

For the 2009/10 Season Italian dance and fitness wear company Freddy has partnered with The Royal Ballet to become official sponsor and supplier of dance fitness wear for the Company. Together they have created the Freddy Royal Ballet Dancers Collection, unique to the dancers, and a Freddy Royal Ballet collection available in Freddy stores worldwide, the Royal Opera House Shop, and online. The collection includes jackets, leggings, towels, a range of bags and accessories, and exclusive souvenir t-shirts. Visit www.freddy.it or www.roh.org.uk/rbshop

Royal Ballet Principal Mara Galeazzi models some of the exclusive Freddy Royal Ballet Dancers' Collection.

Freddy

FREDDY